5OO ANIMALS IN CLAY

500 ANIMALS IN CLAY

CONTEMPORARY EXPRESSIONS OF THE ANIMAL FORM

LARK
BOOKS

A Division of
Sterling Publishing Co., Inc.
New York / London

EDITOR: **Suzanne J.E. Tourtillott**

DESIGNER: **Jackie Kerr**

COVER DESIGNER: **Barbara Zaretsky**

ASSOCIATE EDITOR: **Nathalie Mornu**

ASSOCIATE ART DIRECTOR: **Shannon Yokeley**

ART PRODUCTION ASSISTANT: **Jeff Hamilton**

EDITORIAL ASSISTANCE: **Dawn Dillingham, Delores Gosnell, Rosemary Kast**

EDITORIAL INTERNS: **Megan Taylor Cox, Sue Stigleman**

FRONT COVER
Kelly Connole
Dot, 2005

BACK COVER, CLOCKWISE FROM TOP LEFT
Peter Rose
Bird in Hand, 2003

Ron Mazanowski
Rhino Pot, 1991

Asia Mathis
Unicorn in Foward Fold, 2005

Laura O'Donnell
Fish Plate, 2004

SPINE
Hwang Jeng-daw
Cock Teapot, 2004

FRONT FLAP
Lisa Clague
In the Nature of Things, 2004

BACK FLAP
Yoona Welling
Quoll, 1997–2005

PAGE 3
Marie-Elena Ottman
Quarrelers/Peleones, 2004

PAGE 5
Bryan Hiveley
Goats on Parade, 2005

Library of Congress Cataloging-in-Publication Data

500 animals in clay : contemporary expressions of the animal form / editor, Suzanne J.E. Tourtillott.
     p. cm.
  Includes index.
   ISBN 1-57990-757-1 (pbk.)
  1. Pottery craft. 2. Animals in art. I. Tourtillott, Suzanne J. E. II. Title: Five hundred animals in clay.
TT920.A125 2006
666'.68--dc22

                                        2006015071

10 9 8 7 6 5 4 3

Published by Lark Books, A Division of
Sterling Publishing Co., Inc.
387 Park Avenue South, New York, N.Y. 10016

Text © 2006, Lark Books
Photography © as noted

Distributed in Canada by Sterling Publishing,
c/o Canadian Manda Group, 165 Dufferin Street
Toronto, Ontario, Canada M6K 3H6

Distributed in the United Kingdom by GMC Distribution Services,
Castle Place, 166 High Street, Lewes, East Sussex, England BN7 1XU

Distributed in Australia by Capricorn Link (Australia) Pty Ltd.,
P.O. Box 704, Windsor, NSW 2756 Australia

If you have questions or comments about this book, please contact:
Lark Books, 67 Broadway, Asheville, NC 28801 • (828) 253-0467

Manufactured in China

ISBN 13: 978-1-57990-757-0
ISBN 10: 1-57990-757-1

For information about custom editions, special sales, premium and corporate purchases, please contact Sterling Special Sales Department at 800-805-5489 or specialsales@sterlingpub.com.

Contents

Clay Body, Animal Spirit

Contemporary ceramics is densely rich in animal imagery. Animals are powerful symbols, surrogates for the human psyche; their totemic power endures. Humans covet the dominant and particular attributes of individual species, and at an elemental level we communicate our approbation with names of persons (Wolf Blitzer, Tiger Woods), groups (the Chicago Bears and Bulls, the Baltimore Orioles), and even things (Ford Mustang, Puma shoes). Of course not all animals have our admiration; think of weasels, skunks, snakes, rats, and buzzards.

Whether loved or loathed, feared or esteemed, animals appear in art precisely because of their attributes. I am reminded of a particularly wonderful Peruvian pot, from the Moche culture, that shows fishermen desperately trying to escape a shark attack, and another that portrays a jaguar devouring a man. What could be more magnificent than Han and Tang sculptures of horses and camels? Or the wit and sweetness of a small Greek perfume bottle in the shape of a pig? Any survey of world ceramics reveals the enduring art of animal imagery, past and present.

Some 30,000 years ago—maybe earlier—people in France painted and etched animals on the cave walls of Chauvet-Pont-d'Arc; similar images at Lascaux were made perhaps 10 or 15 millennia later. Some of these pictures were drawn, with a wood-charcoal stump, in a clay ground that covers the stone. They may be the very first clay animals.

The cave drawings are unbelievably beautiful, and more than mere observations; they invoke the spirit of the animals and must have had powerful meaning for their makers. We humans have been enthralled with animals at least since those Paleolithic times: there's a fabulous gallery in the Vatican museum called the Animal Rooms where animal sculptures from Roman antiquity abound. Animals have universal appeal as artistic subject matter and, through time, they occur in all the art forms.

Artists continue to create art with animal themes and figures for much the same reasons that, seemingly, have always motivated them. Early in the last century, Jean Arp, Alexander Calder, Franz Marc, and Pablo Picasso, for example, created masterpieces with animals as central subjects. Among contemporary artists are many whose work exploits the power of animals to convey profound content.

The work in *500 Animals in Clay: Contemporary Expressions of the Animal Form* represents the best contemporary work from an international roster of ceramic artists. In selecting this work I was not surprised by the excellence of craft and execution; in the last couple of decades it has become a standard in ceramics. In any case, I am always more interested in content than technique, and I love pottery as much as figurative sculpture. In fact, the relationship of animal imagery and form to pottery—the food connection—is fundamental. For example, a fish-shaped oval platter used to offer grilled tuna is a familiar visual double-entendre.

Joe Bova
Rabbit Rhyton | 2005
7 X 3½ X 6½ INCHES (17.8 X 8.9 X 16.5 CM)
Modeled and thrown stoneware; electric fired, cone 6
PHOTO © MIKE SMITH

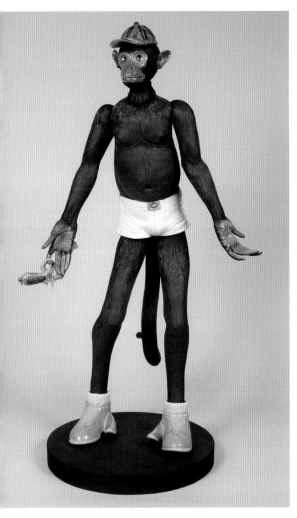

Joe Bova

Gun Monkey II | 2005

35½ X 22 X 16 INCHES (90.2 X 55.9 X 40.6 CM)
Modeled and thrown stoneware; electric fired,
cone 6; china paint, luster overglaze, multi-fired,
cone 018 to cone 015; paint, steel

PHOTO © MIKE SMITH

Regardless of the form, clay artists are using animal imagery to express an abundance of creative ideas. Their works expose human foibles, make political and social commentary, and celebrate the grace and dignity of wild things. Human-animal hybrids—sphinxes, chimeras, and such—abound. Powerful metaphors, similes, and narratives are employed by many of the artists whose work is shown here, such as Bev Hogg's *Salt Stock 3*, Maryann Webster's *Night Sea*, and Logan Wood's *Symbiosis*. Extensions of major art theories, from surrealism and expressionism to beyond postmodernism, are evident as well (see Red Weldon Sandlin's *A Little Lesson in Gravitea* and Lisa Clague's *In the Nature of Things*, for example).

Ceramics sometimes echoes its sister art forms. Works can be found related to cultural/multicultural theory (Laura DeAngelis's *Twin Sisters*) and identity politics (Tré Arenz's *Bernadette of Lourdes*, Elizabeth Zacher's *Pasteurella*, and the installation work of Cynthia Consentino). Other examples, such as Skuja Braden's *Chick* and David Regan's *Cow Drinking*, represent issues of post-colonialism and globalization. Finally, John Byrd's *Squirrel* and spectatorship have something in common. Such works encompass a range of style and content that is, in sum, eclectic.

While not ubiquitous, naturalism as a means of representation is most evident in the work of Karen Copensky, Pamela Earnshaw Kelly, and Michelle C. Gallagher. I was impressed with the ardent interest that animals evoke in clay artists. The empathetic understanding embodied in much of this work is deeply affecting without any condescending sentimentality. Other works, such as those of Beth Cavener Stichter and Dawn Oakford, achieve poignancy with adroit manipulation of material or formal elements, especially color and pattern. Ceramic glazes offer the artist color, surface, and luminosity unique to the medium, unattainable in many others. There are masterly examples to be found in the included work: Emily Dyer's *Lizard Bowl*, Elissa Armstrong's *Orange Lamb*, and Suzy Birstein's *Vase Duet: My Baby Just Cares for Me*. Some artists' remarks, which shed light on their process and inspiration, are included, as well as occasional comments from me.

Animals are important in art because they are important in our lives. In this book you will see how clay artists, through animal imagery, have been inspired to express many of our essential and deepest human experiences. You will find example after example where the content of the art is more than merely animal subject matter.

I acknowledge and appreciate the generosity of every artist who submitted work for consideration and offer congratulations to those who are included. I want to thank Suzanne J.E. Tourtillott, editor, for the opportunity to work on this project, and to her and Nathalie Mornu, associate editor, my thanks for their good humor, patience, and help. My gratitude extends widely to students I have taught since 1970. I have learned much from them too.

— Joe Bova

Joe Bova
Dog Rhyton | 2005

6½ X 7½ X 9 INCHES (16.5 X 19 X 22.9 CM)
Modeled and thrown stoneware and porcelain; electric fired, cone 6
PHOTO © MIKE SMITH

Christopher A. Vicini

Elephant Box | 2003–2004

9 X 18 X 7 INCHES (22.9 X 45.7 X 17.8 CM)

Hand-built stoneware; glaze;
electric fired, cone 5

PHOTO © MARK JOHNSTON

Expressive and redolent, this Chimp *was sculpted by Bill Evans with potent traditional modeling. It's an example of clay's ability to convey life forms vividly when the artist's skills are equal to his or her insight. —JB*

Bill Evans

Chimp | 2005

12 X 8 X 10 INCHES (30.5 X 20.3 X 25.4 CM)
Hand-built stoneware; gas fired,
cone 6; slip, soda fired

PHOTOS © TOM HOLT

11

David Regan's poignant Cow Drinking *could be considered a "green" piece.*
Rife with shades of meaning, it illustrates an aspect of what is mad in this world. —JB

David Regan

Cow Drinking | 2001

16 X 22 INCHES (40.6 X 55.9 CM)
Porcelain
PHOTO COURTESY OF GARTH CLARK GALLERY, NY

Adrian Arleo

Blue Dog | 2005

27½ X 12½ X 14½ INCHES (69.9 X 31.8 X 36.8 CM)

Coil-built, press molded, and altered low-fire
sculpture clay body; electric fired, cone 05

PHOTOS © CHRIS AUTIO
COURTESY OF PACINI LUBEL GALLERY

13

Debbie Fong

Mr. Wrinkles | 2005

8 X 3½ X 9 INCHES (20.3 X 8.9 X 22.9 CM)
Wheel-thrown, altered and assembled;
raku fired

PHOTO © SAADI SHAPIRO AND DAR FONG

Kelly Connole

Dot | 2005

24 X 16 X 9 INCHES (61 X 40.6 X 22.9 CM)
Coil-built stoneware; electric fired,
cone 6; underglazes, glazes
PHOTO © ARTIST

Bill Evans

Black Horse | 2005

13 X 5 X 18 INCHES (33 X 12.7 X 45.7 CM)

Hand-built terra cotta; gas fired in reduction,
cone 06; slips, raku fired

PHOTOS © TOM HOLT

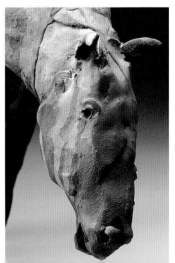

> My attention is drawn to the absurd and the extreme, leading me to concentrate on certain breeds. I enjoy playing with proportions, over-emphasizing heads, shortening legs, and simplifying lines. —KJ

Kerry Jameson

Sitting Bull Terrier with Coat | 2000

16⅛ X 11 X 11 INCHES (41 X 28 X 28 CM)
Hand-coiled earthenware; electric fired, 1100°F
(593°C); slips, glaze, 1060°F (571°C)

PHOTO © HOWIE

Albino baboon or ghost? Glaze and crazing work well to evoke both in this piece by Brenda Bennett. —JB

Brenda Bennett

Baboon | 2004

2¾ X 3½ X 2 INCHES (7 X 9 X 5 CM)
Hand-built white raku; raku fired, cone 06
PHOTO © GARY WEX

Amourentia Louisa Leibman

Leaf Keepers | 2004

ABOVE LEFT, 7 X 5½ X 9 INCHES (17.8 X 14 X 22.9 CM);
ABOVE RIGHT, 7½ X 5½ X 9¼ INCHES (17.8 X 12.7 X 22.9 CM)

Thrown and hand-molded grogged high-fire clay; raku-fired lid, cone 04; electric- and smoke-fired body, cone 017; burnished, terra sigillata

PHOTOS © LOUISA LEIBMAN

Beth Cavener Stichter

Outside, Looking In | 2003

9 X 9½ X 8 INCHES (22.9 X 24.1 X 20.3 CM)

Porcelain, Mason stain

PHOTO © ARTIST

If the word "clayerly" was equivalent to painterly, this piece would win the prize. Patricia Uchill Simons's Orangutan *emits pathos and elicits empathy.* —JB

Patricia Uchill Simons

Orangutan | 2004

14 X 14 X 13 INCHES (35.6 X 35.6 X 33 CM)
Hand-built and wheel-thrown stoneware; electric fired, cone 02; glazes, cone 05
PHOTO © P.K. LOUVE

David Cooke

Macaws | 2005

55 1/8 X 19 11/16 X 15 3/4 INCHES (140 X 50 X 40 CM)
Hand built, coil built, and slab built;
crank, 2282°F (1250°C); oxides, stains

PHOTO © JONATHAN LYNCH

Robin Duke Rodgers

Jungle Jar | 2005

HEIGHT, 18 INCHES (45.7 CM)
Wheel-thrown white stoneware; raku fired,
cone 06; incised, sculpted

PHOTO © GLENN JOHNSON

Alison Palmer

hybrid hen jar | 2005

9½ X 6½ X 5¼ INCHES (24.1 X 16.5 X 13.3 CM)

Thrown and altered stoneware; wood fired, cone 10; glaze

PHOTO © STEVE KATZ

Deborah Johnston
On Top of the World | 2005

6¹¹/₁₆ X 4²/₃ INCHES (17 X 11 CM)
Thrown and sculpted porcelain;
raku fired; copper wire

Kevin B. Hardin
The Warning | 2003

8 X 7 X 4 INCHES (20.3 X 17.8 X 10.2 CM)
Hand-built stoneware; electric fired,
cone 6; painted patina

Clearly, these bully boys appear to be listening to their master's voice. Kerry Jameson's casual approach to surface and glaze finish energizes the compact forms. —JB

Kerry Jameson

Two Sitting Bull Terriers | 2004

14⅛ X 10¼ X 8⅔ INCHES (36 X 26 X 22 CM)
Coil-built grogged buff; electric fired, 1100°F (593°C);
slips, glaze, 1060°F (571°C)

PHOTO © HOWIE

Diane Gilbert

Cat Nap | 2005

7½ X 40 X 23 INCHES (19.1 X 101.6 X 58.4 CM)

Coil and slab-built mixed color clay; electric fired, cone 6; copper carbonate, clear glaze

PHOTOS © KIM KIM FOSTER

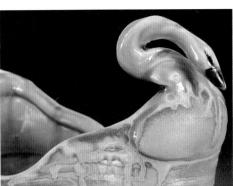

Silvie Granatelli

Swan Moon Bowl | 2002

9 X 18 X 7 INCHES (22.9 X 45.7 X 17.8 CM)
Wheel-thrown and altered porcelain;
gas fired, cone 10

PHOTOS © TIM BARNWELL

Karen Copensky

Trophy Vase | 2004

18 X 9 X 8 INCHES (45.7 X 22.9 X 20.3 CM)

Coil-built and pinched stoneware; anagama fired, natural glaze, cone 12

PHOTO © CRAIG PHILIPS

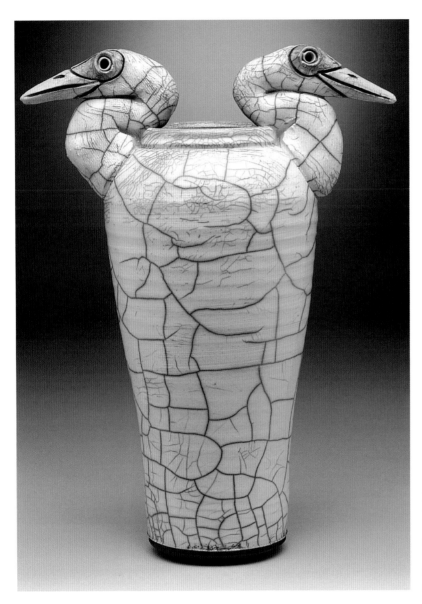

Robin Duke Rodgers

White Egret Effigy Vase | 2005

HEIGHT, 16 INCHES (40.6 CM)
Wheel-thrown white stoneware;
raku fired, cone 06; sculpted

PHOTO © GLENN JOHNSON

Cynthia Bringle
Vase with Turtles | 2004

7 X 8 INCHES (17.8 X 20.3 CM)
Thrown and carved porcelain; soda fired
PHOTO © ARTIST

Karen Copensky
Tripod Warthog Bowl | 2003

8½ X 5½ INCHES (21.6 X 14 CM)
Thrown and pinch-built stoneware;
anagama fired
PHOTO © CRAIG PHILIPS

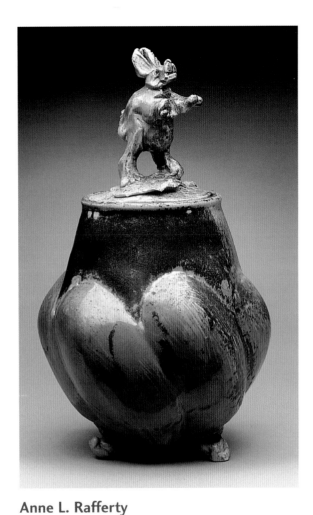

Anne L. Rafferty

Mr. McGregor's Trophy | 2005

10 X 6 X 6 INCHES (25.4 X 15.2 X 15.2 CM)

Thrown, altered and hand-built porcelain;
cone 10; flashing slip, glaze

PHOTO © WALKER MONTGOMERY

Karen Copensky

Twisted Gazelle with Leopard Top | 2004

14¼ X 8¼ X 6 INCHES (36.2 X 21 X 15.2 CM)

Coil-built and pinched stoneware;
anagama fired, cone 10

PHOTO © CRAIG PHILIPS

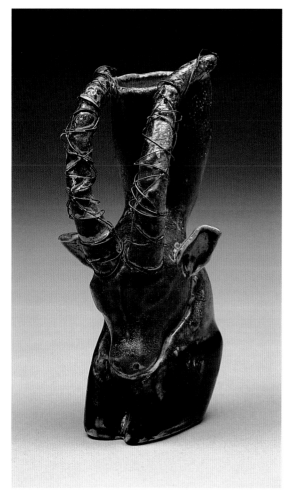

I am intrigued by the idea of animals as power totems. Antelopes represent speed and the adaptability of the mind. I love the way this cup precariously sits on the hoof/saucer, forcing the user to drink with thought and care. —AL

Amy Lenharth

Antelope Cup and Saucer | 2005

5 X 2 X 2 INCHES (12.7 X 5.1 X 5.1 CM)

Slip-cast porcelain; gas fired in reduction, cone 9, cone 10; shino glaze, high-fire wire

PHOTO © JANET RYAN

Joy Lappin

Spirit Keeper | circa 2000

HEIGHT, 12 INCHES (30.5 CM)

Wheel-thrown and hand-sculpted stoneware; bisque
fired, cone 06; luster, multi-fired, cone 06; raku

PHOTOS © TONY DECK

Gillian McMillan's modest pot simply and honestly recalls at least two antecedents: the bird beak-spouted jugs of early Italian majolica as well as colonial Pennsylvanian salt-glazed pottery. —JB

Gillian McMillan

Salt-Glazed Jugbird | 2004

6½ X 7½ X 3½ INCHES (16.5 X 19.1 X 8.9 CM)
Wheel-thrown and assembled stoneware;
ombu kiln, cone 10; salt glazed

PHOTO © EDMOND FONG

Elke Brenning Seefeldt

Bird | 2004

9¼ X 5½ X 5½ INCHES (23.5 X 14 X 14 CM)

Pinched, coiled, and burnished stoneware;
electric fired, cone 010; saggar fired, cone 010

PHOTO © ARTIST

Anne Fallis Elliott

Three Alligator Pitchers | 2000

4 X 7½ X 3½ INCHES (10.2 X 19.1 X 8.9 CM)

Wheel-thrown, altered, and assembled;
electric fired, cone 7; ash glazed

PHOTO © KEVIN NOBLE

This piece was inspired by cherry leaves, and reflects a fascination with the folklore implied by the double-entendre of the title. —BK

Beth Kennedy

The Cock Ate the Cherries | 2003

12 X 12 X 12 INCHES (30.5 X 30.5 X 30.5 CM)
Coil-built, extruded and pinched low-fire
white talc; electric fired, cone 03; wire
PHOTO © TOM FERRIS

Suzy Birstein

Vase Duet: My Baby Just Cares for Me | 2005

6 X 5 X 4 INCHES (15.2 X 12.7 X 10.2 CM)

Hand-built whiteware; electric fired,
cone 01; underglazes, glazes,
acrylic paint, bindhis, cone 04

PHOTOS © KENJI NGAI

This monkey by Scott Causey might be in the business of simian couture. Its surface design, through glaze selection and control, is evocative. —JB

Scott Causey

Monkey | 2005

28 X 22 X 14 INCHES (71.1 X 55.9 X 35.6 CM)

Slip-cast white earthenware;
electric fired, cone 05½; multi-fired,
cone 06; lusters, cone 018; epoxy

PHOTO © ARTIST

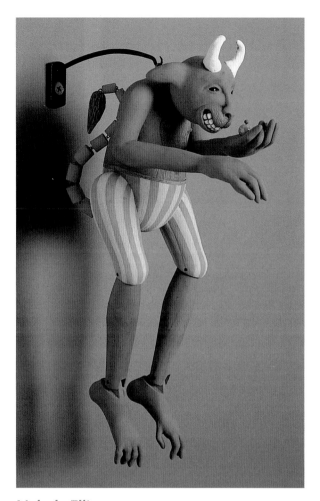

Melody Ellis

Fiend | 2005

9½ X 3¼ X 6 INCHES (24.1 X 8.3 X 15.2 CM)
Hand-built earthenware; electric fired,
cone 04; steel pins, steel hanger

PHOTO © ARTIST

Alan Potter

Lead Foot | 2005

8 X 7 X 5 INCHES (20.3 X 17.8 X 12.7 CM)
Hand-built raku clay; raku fired, cone 06

PHOTO © CHRISTOPHER MARCHETTI PHOTOGRAPHY

I've always been both creeped out by, and fascinated with, bugs and animals. —WLS

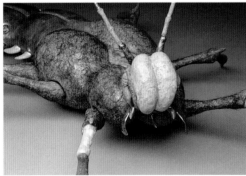

Wesley L. Smith
Arachnoid | 2000

8 X 12 X 26 INCHES (20.3 X 30.5 X 66 CM)
Slab- and coil-built white stoneware; electric fired, cone 04; glaze, luster, enamel paint, human hair

PHOTOS © ARTIST

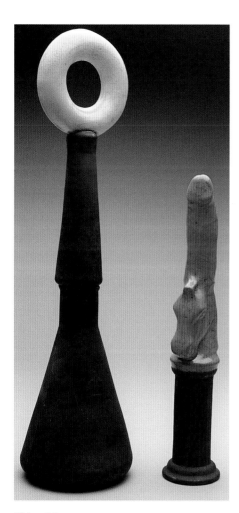

Wes Harvey

He Can't Reach It | 2005

15 X 9 X 6 INCHES (38.1 X 22.9 X 15.2 CM)

Slip-cast porcelain; raku fired, cone 06

Dale Shuffler

Bug Rulers | 1999

LEFT, 14 X 3 X 4 INCHES (35.6 X 7.6 X 10.2 CM);
RIGHT, 9 X 5 X 4 IN. (22.9 X 12.7 X 10.2 CM)

Mold-pressed, coiled, and hand-formed
terra cotta; electric fired, cone 04; black
copper wash on bisque, glaze, terra sigillata

The position of the thylacine/Tasmanian tiger's head was inspired by The Fate of Animals, *a painting by Franz Marc. The last thylacine died in captivity in 1936.* —DO

Dawn Oakford

Thylacine Jug | n.d.

3 15/16 X 7 7/8 X 2 3/4 INCHES (10 X 20 X 7 CM)

Slip-cast stoneware; electric fired,
2300°F (1260°C); underglaze, clear glaze

PHOTO © UFFE SCHULZE

Marlen Moggach

Merganzer and Loon | 2005

TALLEST, 7 X 4½ X 8½ INCHES (17.8 X 11.4 X 21.6 CM)

Wheel-thrown and hand-built raku clay;
cone 06; crackle glaze

PHOTOS © LAURENCE BRUNDRETT

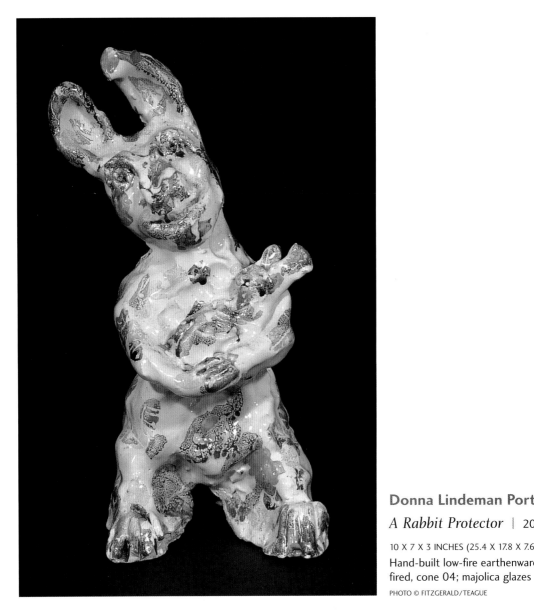

Donna Lindeman Porter

A Rabbit Protector | 2004

10 X 7 X 3 INCHES (25.4 X 17.8 X 7.6 CM)

Hand-built low-fire earthenware; electric fired, cone 04; majolica glazes

PHOTO © FITZGERALD/TEAGUE

Amy M. Santoferraro

Road Show Prop #SRJ93573 | 2004

3 X 4 X 3 INCHES (7.6 X 10.2 X 7.6 CM)

Slip-cast porcelain; electric fired,
cone 6; decals, cone 018

PHOTO © ARTIST

Refined and stylized, Shirley Cristina Usher's somewhat comic turquoise rhino has connotations of Egyptian antecedents—it might be a child's toy or a cult's votive. —JB

Shirley Cristina Usher

Rhino | 2005

12 X 25 X 15 INCHES (30.5 X 63.5 X 38.1 CM)
Coil-built paper clay; electric fired, cone 6
PHOTO © COURTNEY FRISSE

Accumulations of slip-cast animals reflect the culture of acquisition and display of possessions, while my animal-welfare subtext questions the care, use, and detainment of animals. —WW

Wendy Walgate

Ahimsa Trophy Blue | 2005

20 X 9 X 9 INCHES (50.8 X 22.9 X 22.9 CM)
Slip-cast white earthenware; glaze,
cone 06; vintage ceramic container

PHOTOS © ARTIST

Washington Ledesma

Bullet Fish | 2003

24 X 14 X 8 INCHES (61 X 35.6 X 20.3 CM)

Thrown and hand built; electric fired in oxidation,
cone 02; underglazes, sgrafitto, matte finish

PHOTO © JERRY ANTHONY

Comic and erotic by turns, Elephant Rider Teapot, *by Richard Swanson, exploits the sensuality of an unglazed clay surface. Although red, it recalls the same beauty of surface found in the basalt ware of Wedgwood.* —JB

Richard Swanson
Elephant Rider Teapot | 1991

11 X 5½ X 11 INCHES (27.9 X 14 X 27.9 CM)
Cast and sanded fine-grained high-iron clay; bisque fired, cone 06; fired until vitreous, cone 5
PHOTO © ARTIST

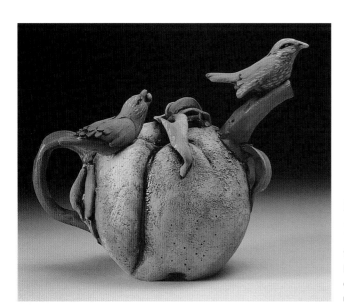

Susan Bostwick
The Offering | 1996

9 X 8 X 6 INCHES (22.9 X 20.3 X 15.2 CM)
Hand-built earthenware; electric fired, cone 04; slips, stains, glaze, multi-fired
PHOTO © JOSEPH GRUBER

Anne L. Rafferty

If Camels Could Fly... | 2005

16 X 17 X 6 INCHES (40.6 X 43.2 X 15.2 CM)

Thrown and assembled white stoneware;
anagama wood-fired, cone 13

PHOTO © WALKER MONTGOMERY

I always breathe into my creatures' noses when they are ready for drying. So much of me is already in them; it feels good to breathe them to life. —ND

Nancy Dimock

A Toast to Me! | 2002

5 X 4 X 11 INCHES (12.7 X 10.2 X 27.9 CM)
Hand-built stoneware; electric fired, bisque, cone 1; acrylic paint

PHOTOS © ALANE L. LESINSKI
COURTESY OF ENCHANTED EARTHENWORKS GALLERY, TUCSON, AZ

Richard Nickel

Lumpy Hill | 2000

21 X 21 X 4 INCHES (53.3 X 53.3 X 10.2 CM)

Hand-built earthenware; electric fired,
cone 04; Mason stains

PHOTO © ARTIST

Norman D. Holen

Guinea Hen | 1967

11½ X 14⅜ X 6¾ INCHES (29.2 X 36.5 X 17.1 CM)
Press-molded earthenware; electric fired, cone 4
PHOTO © PETER LEE

> *I come from Long Island, New York, so this piece was named* Cuckoo Boid *instead of "Cuckoo Bird" to emphasize an accent that some people forever tease me about.* —SO

Stephanie Osser

Cuckoo Boid | 2003

5 X 4 X 5 INCHES (12.7 X 10.2 X 12.7 CM)
White stoneware clay; soda fired,
cone 10; slip, glaze
PHOTO © COREY SILKEN

Vanessa Villarreal

Sanctuary | 2005

7½ X 7 X 1½ INCHES (19.1 X 17.8 X 3.8 CM)

Hand-built porcelain; electric fired, cone 6, cone 06

PHOTO © ARTIST

Wes Harvey

Horse with Ring | 2005

10 X 6 X 6 INCHES (25.4 X 15.2 X 15.2 CM)

Slip-cast porcelain; electric fired, cone 04

PHOTO © ARTIST

Laura McKibbon

Giraffe Platter | 2005

14 X 8 X 1 INCHES (35.6 X 20.3 X 2.5 CM)

Slab-built terra cotta; electric fired, cone 04;
silkscreened underglaze transfer

PHOTO © ARTIST

Yoona Welling

Quoll | 1997–2005

2 X 2 X 3½ INCHES (5 X 5 X 9 CM)

Slip-cast stoneware; electric fired,
cone 8; raw fired, wax resist

PHOTO © UFFE SCHULZE

Keri Huber

Brown Bird on Branch | 2004

2¼ X 2½ X 2¼ INCHES (5.7 X 6.4 X 5.7 CM)

Hand-built earthenware; electric fired, cone 04;
terra sigillata, stain, soda fired, cone 04

PHOTO © JERRY MATHIASON

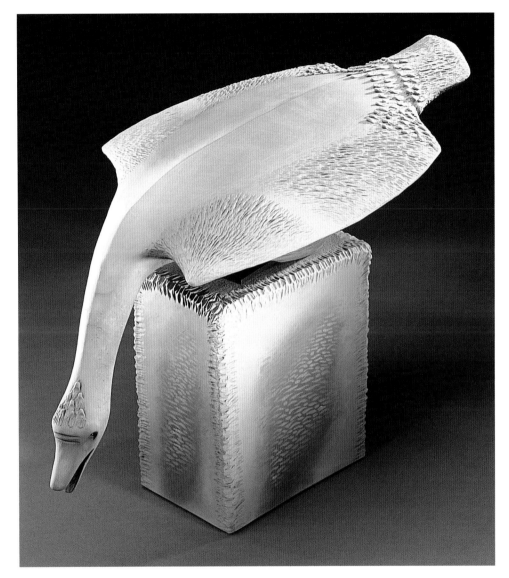

France Fauteux

Rebuff | 2002

24 X 17 X 29 INCHES (61 X 43.2 X 73.7 CM)
Coil-built earthenware; engobe; electric fired, cone 02
PHOTO © GUY COUTURE

Bruce Grimes

Raku Koi-Covered Jar | 2003

13 X 9 INCHES (33 X 22.9 CM)
Wheel-thrown stoneware;
electric fired, cone 06; raku fired
PHOTO © MEL MITTER MILLER

Leslie Green

Cat | 1992

15 X 12½ X 12½ INCHES (38.1 X 31.8 X 31.8 CM)

Slab- and coil-built stoneware; gas fired, cone 6

PHOTO © GARY G. GIBSON

Swan Morningstar Whigham

Ebb Tide | 2005

12¼ X 16¼ X 8¼ INCHES (31.1 X 41.3 X 21 CM)

Hand-built stoneware; salt fired, cone 3

PHOTOS © WALKER MONTGOMERY

Dennis Sipiorski

Gator Teapot | 2000

12 X 12 X 9 INCHES (30.5 X 30.5 X 22.9 CM)
Thrown and built low-fire red clay; slip,
low fired; salt fired

PHOTO © ARTIST

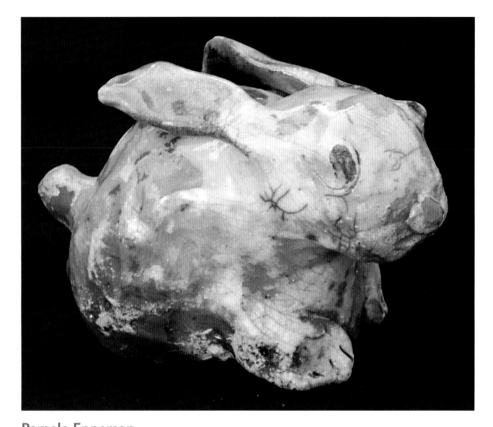

Pamela Epperson
Raku Rabbit | 2004

4 X 6 X 4 INCHES (10.2 X 15.2 X 10.2 CM)
Hand-built raku clay; raku fired, cone 03
PHOTO © EDWIN COX

Brian McArthur

Rabbit Casserole | 1999

9 X 14 X 8 INCHES (22.9 X 35.6 X 20.3 CM)
Thrown and slab-built stoneware; salt fired, cone 10
PHOTO © ARTIST

Susan Greenleaf

Untitled | 1992

26 X 15 X 12 INCHES (66 X 38.1 X 30.5 CM)
Wheel-thrown and altered stoneware;
glaze, cone 10

PHOTO © RICHARD RODRIQUEZ

Susan Bostwick

Drawing Fire | 2002

13 X 7 X 6 INCHES (33 X 17.8 X 15.2 CM)

Hand-built earthenware; electric fired,
cone 03; slips, stains, glazes

PHOTOS © JOSEPH GRUBER

Jaimie Cooney

Internal Raven | 2003

29 X 20 X 16 INCHES (73.7 X 50.8 X 40.6 CM)

Slab- and hand-built paper clay; electric fired, cone 6

PHOTO © ARTIST

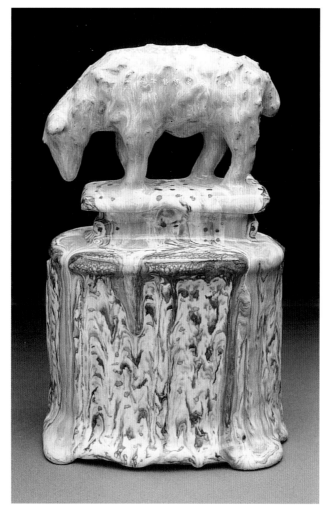

Elissa Armstrong

Orange Lamb | 2004

8 X 5 X 2 INCHES (20.3 X 12.7 X 5.1 CM)
Hand-built earthenware; electric fired,
cone 04; decals, cone 018

PHOTO © ARTIST

Orange Lamb *exhibits the unique and powerful effect of glaze and, whether intended or not, subliminal religious symbolism is evident in this work by Elissa Armstrong.* —JB

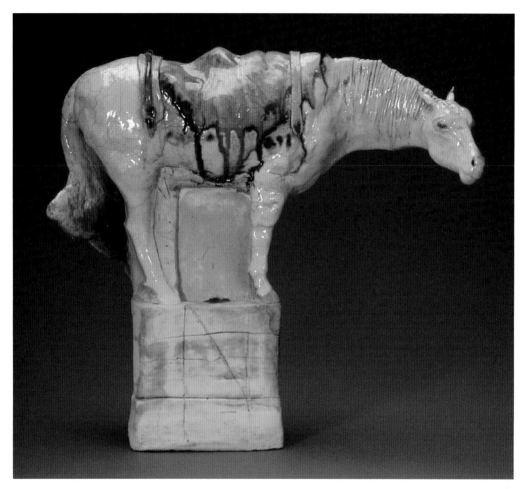

Pamela Earnshaw Kelly

Green Door | 2001

14 X 16 X 9 INCHES (35.6 X 40.6 X 22.9 CM)

Slab-built raku clay; raku fired, cone 05; glaze, slip

PHOTO © ARTIST

Mimicry of Tang glazing and good-old farm horse harnesses suggest this beauty is a time traveler of some sort. —JB

Sue Tirrell

Plow Horse | 2002

14 X 15 X 7 INCHES (35.6 X 38.1 X 17.8 CM)

Slab-built stoneware; wood fired, cone 10

In our home we
often wonder who
really is in charge...this
frilly, overdressed, pam-
pered pet is obviously the
boss here, overturning a
traditional family role
into a reign. —JMW

Janis Mars Wunderlich
Puppy King | 2005

19 X 9 X 16 INCHES (48.3 X 22.9 X 40.6 CM)
Hand-built earthenware; cone 3; slip,
underglaze, overglaze, cone 04
PHOTOS © ARTIST

Mary E. Kershaw

The Adopted Ones from across the Bridge | 2005

14³/₁₆ X 13 X 7½ INCHES (36 X 33 X 19 CM)

Coil-built porcelain mixed with stoneware; electric fired,
cone 8; glazes, oxides

PHOTO © ROBERT J. KERSHAW

Scott Stockdale

Forgive not Forget | 2002

34 X 18 X 14 INCHES (86.4 X 45.7 X 35.6 CM)
Hand-built earthenware; electric fired,
cone 04; polychromed
PHOTOS © ARTIST

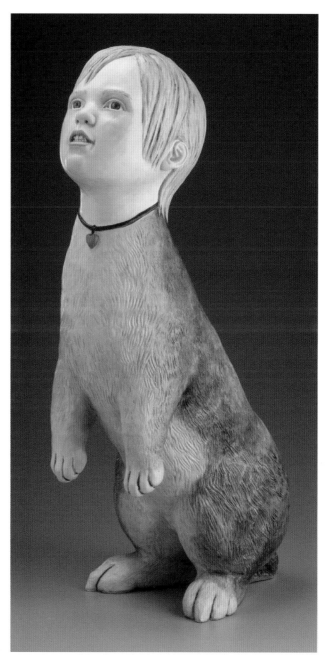

Cynthia Consentino
Rabbit Girl III | 2005

32 X 18 X 13 INCHES (81.3 X 45.7 X 33 CM)
Clay, slip, oils, cold wax
PHOTO © JOHN POLAK

Cynthia Consentino
Rabbit Girl II | 2005

38 X 15½ X 18½ INCHES (96.5 X 39.4 X 47 CM)
Clay, slip, oils, cold wax
PHOTO © JOHN POLAK

Melanie Ann Wegner

You Don't Say! | 2003

21 X 17 X 13 INCHES (53.3 X 43.2 X 33 CM)

Coil-built stoneware; electric fired, cone 6;
underglaze, acrylic paint

PHOTO © MARGOR GIEST

Maryann Webster

Monsanto Pond | 2003

12 X 18 X 7 INCHES (30.5 X 45.7 X 17.8 CM)

Hand-built porcelain and stoneware;
soda fired, cone 9

PHOTO © ARTIST

Kurt Weiser

Navigator | 2000

11 X 16½ INCHES (27.9 X 41.9 CM)

Porcelain

PHOTO © CRAIG SMITH
COURTESY OF GARTH CLARK GALLERY, NY

Clinton Berry

Platter | 2004

18¾ X 4¼ INCHES (47.6 X 10.8 CM)

Stoneware; gas fired in reduction, cone 9

PHOTO © TONY DECK

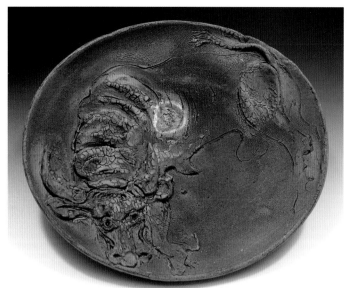

Kenneth Ferguson

Bull Charger | 2003

3 ¾ X 18 ½ INCHES (9.5 X 47 CM)
Black stoneware
PHOTO COURTESY OF GARTH CLARK GALLERY, NY

Jenny Lind

Raven in Winter | 2004

16 X 2 ½ INCHES (40.6 X 6.4 CM)
Thrown white earthenware; electric fired,
cone 3; underglaze, clear glaze
PHOTO © RICHARD FALLER

Patrick L. Dougherty

Toucan | 2004

4 X 24 INCHES (10.2 X 61 CM)
Wheel-thrown white earthenware; electric fired,
cone 04; underglazes, clear glaze
PHOTO © GREG KUCHIK

Marie-Elena Ottman

Unity | 2005

24 X 15 X 11 INCHES (61 X 38.1 X 27.9 CM)

Coil-built earthenware; electric fired, cone 03; slips, underglazes, sgrafitto, wax resist, glaze, cone 04

PHOTO © GEOFFREY CARR PHOTOGRAPHY

Harriet Ann Thompson

Frog with Moon and Stars | 2000

7 X 7 X ¾ INCHES (17.8 X 17.8 X 1.9 CM)

Hand-built flattened terra cotta; electric fired, cone 04; overglaze, cone 06; luster, cone 019

PHOTO © D. KENT THOMPSON

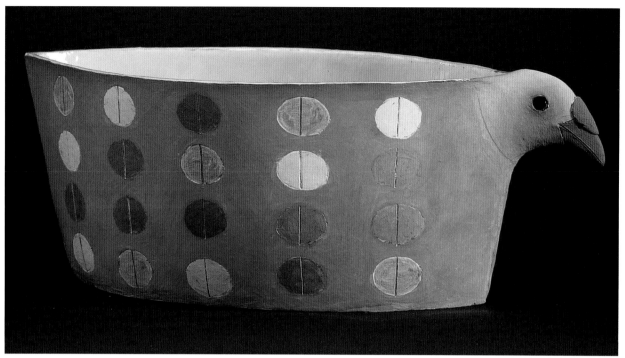

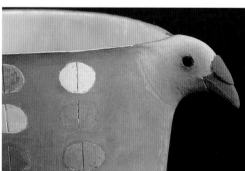

Anne-Beth Borselius

Blue Bird-Vessel | 2004

5½ X 13¾ X 5⁵⁄₁₆ INCHES (14 X 35 X 13.5 CM)

Hand-built earthenware; electric fired, cone 04; slips, burnished, partly glazed

PHOTOS © PEO ERIKSSON

Kate Fisher has made an elegant integration of surface and image. With its koi fish, her Coy Pitcher *evokes Asian as well as European forms.* —JB

Kate Fisher

The Coy Pitcher | 2005

11 X 5 X 5 INCHES (27.9 X 12.7 X 12.7 CM)

Wheel-thrown porcelain; oxidation fired, cone 6; decals, cone 017

PHOTO © STEVE SCHNIEDER

Farraday Newsome

Considering Persephone | 2004

12½ X 11 X 11 INCHES (31.8 X 27.9 X 27.9 CM)
Slab-built and press-molded terra cotta;
electric fired, cone 05; majolica

PHOTO © ARTIST

Color, pattern, and surface decoration combine beautifully in Annette Corcoran's teapot. The loopy, meandering lines on the wing and the crest feather are just the right counterpoint to the geometry of the overall feather patterns. —JB

Annette Corcoran

Red-Headed Woodpecker Teapot | 2003

9¾ X 6½ X 6½ INCHES (24.8 X 16.5 X 16.5 CM)

Thrown and altered porcelain; electric fired, cone 1; underglazes, glazes, overglazes

PHOTO © PATRICK TRAGENZA

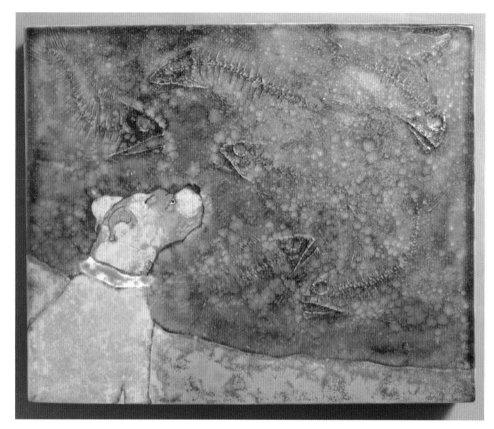

Bruce Gholson

Samantha Henneke

Babu Dreams | 2005

16 X 13¼ X 2½ INCHES (40.6 X 33.7 X 6.4 CM)

Slip-cast porcelain; electric fired, cone 7;
querda seca, slip, molybdenum crystal glazes

PHOTO © BULLDOG POTTERY

I'm interested in creating pieces to be used to display and serve food—and what remains afterward. —JT

James Tingey

Dead Fish Platter | 2005

DIAMETER, 14 INCHES (35.6 CM)

Wheel-thrown porcelain;
gas fired, cone 10; sgraffito

PHOTO © ARTIST

Michael Simon

Persian Jar with Black Fish | 2001

14½ X 7½ X 7½ INCHES (36.8 X 19 X 19 CM)

Wheel-thrown and altered earthenware; salt fired

PHOTO © BARD WRISLEY
COURTESY OF THE SIGNATURE SHOP & GALLERY, ATLANTA, GA

Farraday Newsome

Garden of Ambiguity | 2004

17 X 9½ X 8 INCHES (43.2 X 24.1 X 20.3 CM)

Slab-built and press-molded terra cotta;
electric fired, cone 05; majolica

PHOTO © ARTIST

Cheri Yarnell

Whale Song | 2004

16 X 10 INCHES (40.6 X 25.4 CM)
Wheel thrown and carved earthenware;
smoke fired; terra sigilatta, burnished

PHOTO © DAVID EGAN

Sue Tirrell

Pompeii Rider | 2005

19 X 15 X 7 INCHES (48.3 X 38.1 X 17.8 CM)
Slab-built earthenware; electric fired,
cone 04; terra sigillata, underglazes, lusters
PHOTO © ARTIST

Jaimie Cooney

Divine Equine | 2002

9 X 8 X 3 INCHES (22.9 X 20.3 X 7.6 CM)
Hand-built, low-fire buff clay; electric fired,
cone 04; heesun glaze
PHOTO © ARTIST

*This is based on a bad-tempered and tubby pony
we had as children. As we mounted, he would either
bite our rear or kick out, landing a hefty blow.* —SM

Sue Masters

Pony | 1997

5⅛ X 7½ X 4¾ INCHES (13 X 19 X 12 CM)
Slip-cast earthenware; biscuit fired, 2021°F (1105°C);
glazed, 1897°F (1036°C)
PHOTO © DARYL T. ENEVER

Stylization emphasizes the heroic proportion of this noble horse. Stefani Gruenberg does not exactly quote earlier equestrian masterpieces but certainly offers a nod to historic Chinese as well as modern Italian masters. —JB

Stefani Gruenberg

Dark Horse | 2005

15 X 12 X 4 INCHES (38.1 X 30.5 X 10.2 CM)
Slab-built stoneware; gas fired, cone 8;
crackle glaze, cone 06; metal rods

PHOTO © BILIANA POPOVA

Pamela Earnshaw Kelly

Dream Goat | 2003–2004

13 X 13 X 4 INCHES (33 X 33 X 10.2 CM)
Slab-built raku clay; raku fired,
cone 05; patina, paint
PHOTO © ARTIST

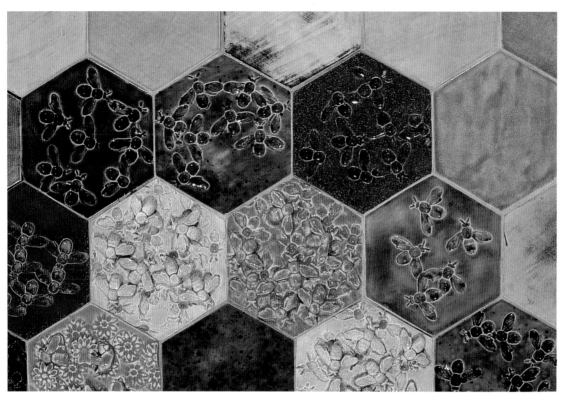

Susan Tunick

Three Times Three (Hexagon #2) | 2002

EACH TILE, 6 INCHES (15.2 CM) ACROSS

Press-molded low-fire white clay;
electric fired, cone 04

PHOTO © PETER MAUSS/ESTO

Samantha Henneke

Red-Eye Fly | 2005

7¾ X 7¾ X 1½ INCHES (19.7 X 19.7 X 3.8 CM)

Slip-cast porcelain; electric fired, cone 7;
querda seca, slip, molybdenum crystal glazes

PHOTO © BULLDOG POTTERY

Ian F. Thomas

Dinner for One | 2005

12 X 12 X ½ INCHES (30.5 X 30.5 X 1.3 CM)

Slab-built terra cotta; cone 04; transfer,
underglaze, stick, glaze, cone 04

PHOTO © ARTIST

> *The quoll, a native cat, is on the list of endangered species in Australia.* —DO

Dawn Oakford

Quoll Jug | n.d.

3 15/16 X 7 7/8 X 2 3/4 INCHES (10 X 20 X 7 CM)

Slip-cast stoneware; electric fired, 2300°F (1260°C); underglaze, clear glaze

PHOTO © JOHN FARROW

Kathleen Laurie

Turtle Tile | 2004

8 X 8 X 1/2 INCHES (20.3 X 20.3 X 1.3 CM)

Slab-built earthenware; electric fired, cone 04; commercial underglazes, gold marker

PHOTO © MAD DOG STUDIO

Mary Ann Charette

Hunting Cheetah | 2002

6 X 11 INCHES (15.2 X 27.9 CM)

Carved porcelain; underglaze;
electric fired, cone 04; smoked

PHOTO © PAUL ELBO

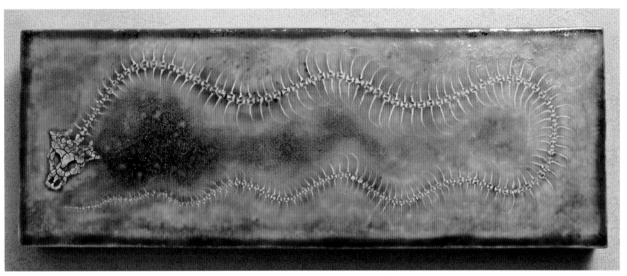

Bruce Gholson

Serpent Fossil | 2005

20¼ X 7½ X 2½ INCHES (51.4 X 19.1 X 6.4 CM)
Slip-cast porcelain; electric fired, cone 7;
molybdenum crystal glazes, slip

PHOTOS © BULLDOG POTTERY

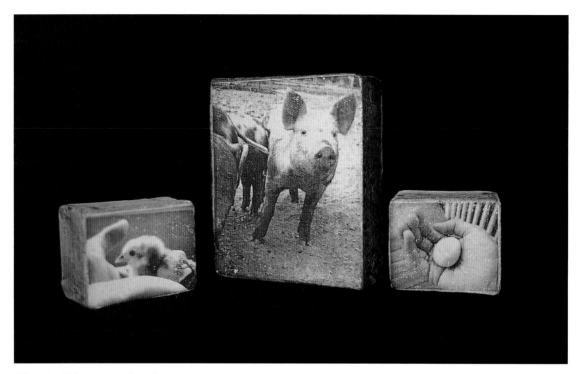

Cherie Westmoreland

Farm Tour | 2005

LEFT: 1¾ X 3 X 1½ INCHES (4.4 X 7.6 X 3.8 CM);
CENTER: 5 X 4 X 1½ IN. (12.7 X 10.2 X 3.8 CM);
RIGHT: 1¾ X 2½ X 1½ IN. (4.4 X 6.4 X 3.8 CM)

Slab-built stoneware; electric fired, cone 6;
laser image transfer; low-fire clear glaze wash;
iron oxide, glazes

PHOTO © ARTIST

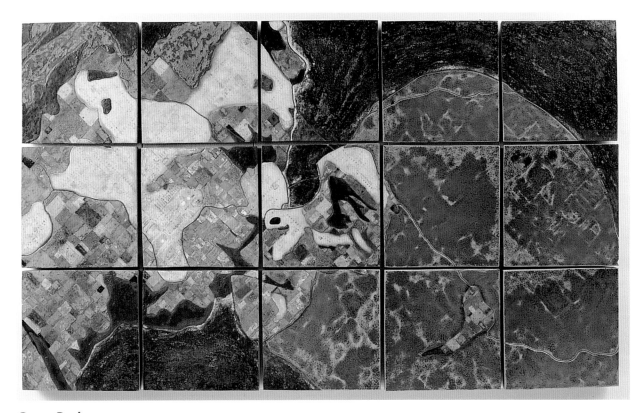

Gary Carlos

The Kiss | 2003

24 X 40 INCHES (61 X 101.6 CM)

Earthenware; electric fired, cone 04; multi-fired

PHOTO © ARTIST

Melody Ellis

Fish Tile | 2003

5 X 5 X ½ INCHES (12.7 X 12.7 X 1.3 CM)

Hand-carved earthenware;
electric fired, cone 04; grout

PHOTO © ARTIST

Debra Bacianga

Dog in the Moonlight | 2005

5½ X 5½ INCHES (14 X 14 CM)

Hand-pressed and molded stoneware;
electric fired, cone 5; glazed

PHOTO © LISA ALHBERG

Mary Ann Charette

Wild Horse Corner | 2002

7 X 10½ INCHES (17.8 X 26.7 CM)
Carved porcelain; underglaze;
electric fired, cone 04; smoked
PHOTOS © PAUL ELBO

Kathy Phelps

Horse Dreams | 2005

2 X 5 X 5 INCHES (5.1 X 12.7 X 12.7 CM)
Wheel-thrown and altered white
stoneware; salt fired,
cone 6; underglaze
PHOTO © WALKER MONTGOMERY

Image, glaze, and pattern conspire to raise timeless questions about life and death in the animal world in Bruce Gholson's Serpent with Fossil Fish. *—JB*

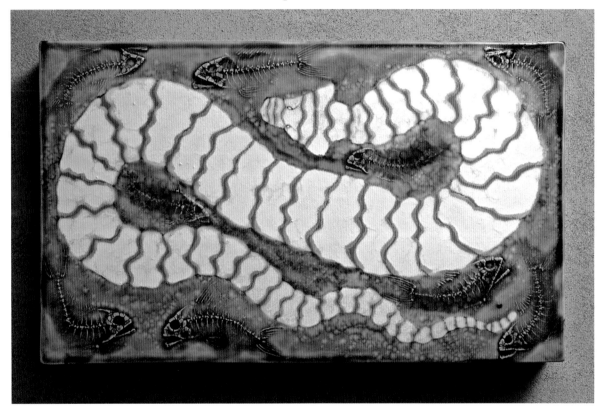

Bruce Gholson

Serpent with Fossil Fish | 2005

18 1/4 X 11 X 2 1/2 INCHES (46.4 X 27.9 X 6.4 CM)
Slip-cast porcelain; electric fired, cone 7;
querda seca, slip, molybdenum crystal glazes
PHOTO © BULLDOG POTTERY

In the thicket, what entices can also entangle and entrap. —CL

Cary Loving

Tangle | 2005

14 X 18 X 4 INCHES (35.6 X 45.7 X 10.2 CM)

Hand-built and extended pinched clay;
low-temperature fired; engobe, glazes, encaustic

PHOTO © ERIC NORBOM

Clive Tucker

Boris Triceratops Head | 1996

22 X 18 X 19 INCHES (55.9 X 45.7 X 48.3 CM)

Solid-built and hollowed stoneware; electric fired, cone 6; oxides, glaze

PHOTOS © PETER HOGAN

Cynthia Siegel

Search | 2003

22 X 14 X 8 INCHES (55.9 X 35.6 X 20.3 CM)

Hand-built, extruded, and altered white stoneware;
electric fired, cone 04; commercial glazes and
underglazes, cone 03; luster, cone 018

PHOTOS © STAN EINHORN AND ARTIST

Sue Whitmore

Buzz-Buzz | 2000

9 X 26 X 26 INCHES (22.9 X 66 X 66 CM)

Hand-built stoneware; electric fired, cone 6, cone 1, cone 04; multifired, engobe, glaze, underglaze

PHOTOS © ARTIST

Maryann Webster

Dioxin Sea | 2005

16 X 29 X 7 INCHES (40.6 X 73.7 X 17.8 CM)

Hand-built and slip-cast porcelain and stoneware; soda fired, cone 6

PHOTO © ARTIST

Sheryl McRoberts

Two Turtles | 2000

14 X 36 INCHES (35.6 X 91.4 CM)

Terra cotta relief

PHOTO © ARTIST

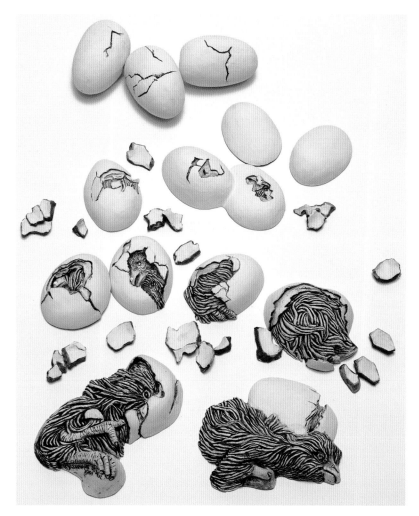

Stephanie Osser

All about Eggs | 2002

23 X 20 X 3 INCHES (58.4 X 50.8 X 7.6 CM)

Molded low-fire slip; underglaze;
electric fired, cone 04

PHOTO © CLIVE RUSS

Dying Reef *refers to the recent dire predictions that, in the next twenty years, the world's coral reefs will be completely destroyed. The loss of this critical habitat will also destroy the animal life dependent on the reef.* —MW

Maryann Webster
Dying Reef | 2004

16 X 5 INCHES (40.6 X 12.7 CM)
Hand-built porcelain and stoneware;
soda fired, cone 9
PHOTO © ARTIST

Mark Chatterley

Crows | 2004

72 X 36 X 36 INCHES (182.9 X 91.4 X 91.4 CM)

Slab-built stoneware; reduction fired,
cone 6; crater glaze

PHOTO © ARTIST

Jack Thompson, AKA Jugo de Vegetales

Gemini | 2004

28 X 25 X 29 INCHES (71.1 X 63.5 X 73.7 CM)

Cast and modeled paper clay; gas fired,
cone 05; graphite, alkyd medium

PHOTO © ARTIST

The intent of my work is to evoke the animal spirit that was once destroyed, and to make amends for the discord and waste. —*LMP*

Lisa Merida-Paytes
Fish Stringer | 2005

36 X 43 X 39 INCHES (91.4 X 109.2 X 99.1 CM)
Coil-built stoneware; electric fired,
cone 05; raku fired, cone 06
PHOTOS © JAY BACHEMIN

Renee Audette

Playthings | 2003

16 X 14 X 4 INCHES (40.6 X 35.6 X 10.2 CM)

Hand-built porcelain; electric fired,
cone 6; fabric, hair, slips, stains

PHOTOS © JOHN KNAUB

The crow is my choice to allegorically depict the confinements of adulthood. Twelve interchangeable crows created from molds appear in a grid format to represent conformity and the loss of identity. —IF

Ilena Finocchi

Harbingers | 2005

10 X 8 X 4 INCHES (25.4 X 20.3 X 10.2 CM)
Slip-cast porcelain; electric fired,
cone 6; lost-wax cast bronze

PHOTOS © GEOFF TESCH

Laurie Sharkus

Singing Whale | 2005

20 X 16 X 12 INCHES (50.8 X 40.6 X 30.5 CM)
Solid, slab-built, hollowed, and coil-built
stoneware clay; electric fired, cone 07;
sawdust fired; painted, smoke fired
PHOTO © ARTIST

The African contingent seems to be in charge, but it is a delicate balance. James Ibur's totem seems to ask, "Who will inherit the earth?" —JB

James Ibur

Ararat | 1994

72 X 48 X 24 INCHES (182.9 X 121.9 X 61 CM)
Coil-built earthenware; cone 04; mixed media; assisted by Gloria Fuchs

PHOTO © MARK KATZMAN

Denise Romecki

Coffee Break | 2001

14 X 21 X 6 INCHES (35.6 X 53.3 X 15.2 CM)
Slab-built and sculpted stoneware; cone 2;
underglaze, glaze, oxides, cone 05

PHOTO © JERRY ANTHONY

Clay is skin, skin is clay; Pamela Earnshaw Kelly's naturalism surpasses mere realism. —JB

Pamela Earnshaw Kelly

Touching the Earth | 2004

12 X 19 X 34 INCHES (30.5 X 48.3 X 86.4 CM)
Slab-built raku clay; raku fired in reduction, cone 05
PHOTO © ARTIST

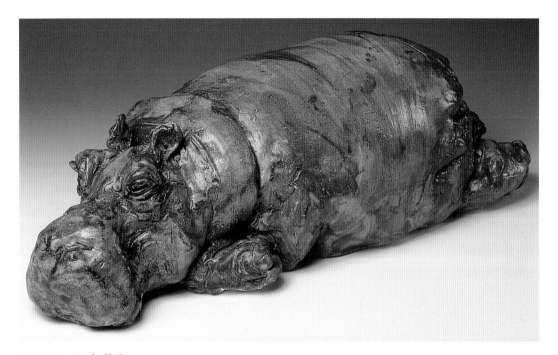

Patricia Uchill Simons

Lying Hippo | 2004

8 X 9 X 22 INCHES (20.3 X 22.9 X 55.9 CM)

Wheel-thrown and hand-built stoneware;
electric fired, cone 02; glazes, cone 05

PHOTO © BOB BARRETT

Pamela Timmons

Iguana | 2001

6 X 12 X 11 INCHES (15.2 X 30.5 X 27.9 CM)

Sculpted stoneware; iron oxide, wash; reduction fired, cone 9

PHOTOS © JIM WOLNOSKY

American Toad on Toadstool, *by Natalie Surving and Richard Surving,*
recalls the virtuosity and realism of Johann Joachim Kaendler's Meissen
animals as well as later European porcelain works. —JB

Natalie Surving
Richard Surving
American Toad on Toadstool | 1986

5 X 5½ X 5 INCHES (12.7 X 14 X 12.7 CM)
Hand-built porcelain; cone 10; airbrushed glaze
PHOTO © RICHARD SURVING

Patti Sandberg

Ag | 2004

8 X 7 X 12 INCHES (20.3 X 17.8 X 30.5 CM)

Hand-built earthenware; cone 04; slips, glazes

PHOTO © ARTIST

Jane Dunsmore

The Tenant Farmer's Cow | 2002

5 X 10 X 6 INCHES (12.7 X 25.4 X 15.2 CM)

Slab-built paper clay; raku fired

PHOTO © DON DUNSMORE
COLLECTION OF ANDREA BURCHETTE

The claws are used cones. —SL

Sylvia Lampen

P.D. | 2005

8 X 4 X 8 INCHES (20.3 X 10.2 X 20.3 CM)

Coil-built low-fire red clay;
electric fired, cone 04; underglaze,
oxides, cone 05

PHOTOS © DAVID GULISANO

Conveying the breakup of the polar ice cap, Molyneaux links environment, event, and animal with a selective application of crackle raku glaze. —JB

Sara Molyneaux

Untitled | 2003

9 X 16 X 8 INCHES (22.9 X 40.6 X 20.3 CM)

Thrown, altered and hand-built grogged stoneware;
raku fired, cone 06; slip, clear glaze

PHOTO © TOM HOLT

Bev Hogg

Salt Stock 3 | 2002

47¼ X 19¹¹⁄₁₆ X 19¹¹⁄₁₆ INCHES (120 X 50 X 50 CM)

Coil-built mid-fire clay; electric fired, cone 6;
engobes, oxides, salt lick mineral block

PHOTOS © BEN HOGG

The cauliflower of Winky's gloves is nearly matched by that of his suffering brow. Clay's capacity for mimicry in the skillful hands of Andrew Davis is here amply evident. —JB

Andrew Davis

Winky the Bear | 2005

16 X 7 X 6 INCHES (40.6 X 17.8 X 15.2 CM)

Hand-built red earthenware;
electric fired, cone 04; terra sigillata;
glaze, cone 06

PHOTO © RACHEL BLEIL

133

Slipstream Dream *is meditative, serene, and beautifully executed by Kevin B. Hardin.* —JB

Kevin B. Hardin

Slipstream Dream | 2005

8½ X 6 X 28 INCHES (21.6 X 15.2 X 71.1 CM)

Hand-built stoneware; electric fired, cone 6; painted patina, copper

PHOTOS © DON WHEELER

Susan Halls

Rooster | 2002

25 9/16 X 10 5/8 X 8 1/4 INCHES (65 X 27 X 21 CM)
Slab-built, pinched, and coil-built paper
clay; raku fired, smoked, cone 07; slip
PHOTO © PATRICK VINGO

Jack Thompson, AKA Jugo de Vegetales

Nacimiento de la Diosa de Maiz | 1999

12 X 20 X 18 INCHES (30.5 X 50.8 X 45.7 CM)

Cast and modeled paper clay; electric fired,
cone 05; pigments, alkyd medium

PHOTO © ARTIST

In my interpretation of the Native American totem pole, the animals come from all over the world instead of just the Pacific Northwest, giving them more of a global meaning. —*MFP*

Marlene Ferrell Parillo
Totem Pole | 2004

22 X 10 X 12 INCHES (55.9 X 25.4 X 30.5 CM)
Hand-built brown stoneware; electric fired,
cone 6; paint, glaze
PHOTO © HOWARD GOODMAN

Nan Jacobsohn

Three Dog Night | 2002

27 X 18 X 12 INCHES (68.6 X 45.7 X 30.5 CM)

Coil-built stoneware; electric fired, cone 6;
smoked, iron oxide

PHOTO © JOHN LUCAS

Betty Ludington's Trio *all seem to have their eyes on the same prize—perhaps a hopping contest. Bracketed and contrasted by his dark neighbors, the frog appears to be in the spotlight. One could imagine him to be the star jumper from Calaveras County.* —JB

Betty Ludington

Trio | 2000

11 X 7 X 11 INCHES (27.9 X 17.8 X 27.9 CM)
Coil-built stoneware; electric fired,
cone 5; underglazes, clear glaze

PHOTO © EMMY JOHNSTON

In the evocative Vermilion River Zodiac, *Chris Berti reveals the secret animal hidden in each brick; his method is a direct link to the early animal symbolism in carvings that ornamented medieval churches.* —JB

Chris Berti

Vermilion River Zodiac | 2005

14 X 15 X 15 INCHES (35.6 X 38.1 X 38.1 CM)
Earthenware brick, fire brick; carved

PHOTOS © ARTIST

Jenny Lind

Horse | 2004

12 X 7 X 14 INCHES (30.5 X 17.8 X 35.6 CM)

Coil-built stoneware; electric fired,
cone 6; underglaze, clear glaze

PHOTO © RICHARD FALLER
COLLECTION OF ALICE GRIFFITH

Ann Roberts

River Riders #6 | 1998

9⁷/₁₆ X 16¹⁵/₁₆ X 7¹/₁₆ INCHES (24 X 43 X 18 CM)

Hollow slab-built, pinched, and hand-built
white earthenware; glaze, cone 02; overglaze,
electric fired, cone 06

PHOTO © ARTIST

Chuck McWeeny

Group Diary | 1993

9 X 11 X 3 INCHES (22.9 X 27.9 X 7.6 CM)
Slip-cast porcelain; soda fired, cone 10;
slip-cast, cone 10

PHOTO © ARTIST

Inspiration for my work derives from historic interpretations of animals, from cave paintings of Lascaux to 18th-century British livestock paintings. —DJ

Delyth Jones

Herd | 2004

4¾ X 1⁹⁄₁₆ X 7⅞ INCHES (12 X 4 X 20 CM)
Slab-built white earthenware; bisque fired,
1976°F (1080°C); smoke fired

PHOTO © ARTIST

Kari Temming

Birds of a Feather | 2005

25 X 18 X 14 INCHES (63.5 X 45.7 X 35.6 CM)

Slip-cast porcelain, electric fired, cone 6; underglaze

PHOTO © ARTIST

Michelle C. Gallagher

Mr. Monk | 1998

21 X 21 X 15 INCHES (53.3 X 53.3 X 38.1 CM)
Hand- and coil-built stoneware; gas fired,
cone 10; oxides, gold leaf
PHOTO © COURTNEY FRISSE

Mary Jordan's Shino Rabbit *is an example of how ceramics can make the mundane imaginative and elevate the incidental to the transformative.* —JB

Mary Jordan
Shino Rabbit | 2005

8½ X 5½ X 9 INCHES (21.6 X 14 X 22.9 CM)
Hand sculpted; wood fired, cone 10; shino glaze
PHOTO © SUE NORRIS

Jean-Pierre Larocque
Untitled Horse | 2003

13 X 15 INCHES (33 X 38.1 CM)
Stoneware
PHOTO © NOEL ALLUM
COURTESY OF GARTH CLARK GALLERY, NY

This is one fine prize-winning sheep by Susan Halls, whose glaze work creates a very fine interpretation of nature. —JB

Susan Halls

Ornamental Sheep in the Staffordshire Style | 2005

6 11/16 X 3 15/16 X 8 2/3 INCHES (17 X 10 X 22 CM)

Press-molded paper clay; raku fired, cone 07

PHOTO © ARTIST

Rena Fafalios's Trojan Turtle *bears the records and marks of what might be the residue of a fabled battle. Its rich surface also suggests a long-ago time when turtles lived with the dinosaurs. —JB*

Rena Fafalios

Trojan Turtle | 2005

4 X 4½ X 8 INCHES (10.2 X 11.4 X 20.3 CM)
Hand-built stoneware; electric fired
in oxidation, cone 6; glaze, wax

PHOTO © D. JAMES DEE

Asymmetry contributes to the gesture and movement in Rhino Ewer. *Karen Copensky magically weds animal to pot with good design and transition of form.* —JB

Karen Copensky

Rhino Ewer | 2004

5 X 4 X 9½ INCHES (12.7 X 10.2 X 24.1 CM)
Coil-built and pinched stoneware;
anagama fired, cone 10

PHOTO © CRAIG PHILIPS

Tré Arenz

King Hoot | 2003

29 X 17 X 15 INCHES (73.7 X 43.2 X 38.1 CM)

Hand-built clay

PHOTO © DAVID WHARTON
COLLECTION OF JOHN MICHAEL KOHLER ART CENTER, SHEBOYGAN, WI
COURTESY OF WILLIAM CAMPBELL CONTEMPORARY ART, INC.

Alison Palmer

goaty thing | 2005

13 X 11 X 7½ INCHES (33 X 27.9 X 19.1 CM)
Thrown and altered white stoneware;
wood fired, cone 10

PHOTO © STEVE KATZ

> The eland is a sacred animal to the Bushman of Africa and thought to endow an individual with supernatural powers and increase communications with the gods. —AL

Amy Lenharth

Eland Rhyton | 2005

16 X 5 X 5 INCHES (40.6 X 12.7 X 12.7 CM)
Thrown and hand-built stoneware; gas and salt fired, cone 9, cone 10

PHOTOS © JANET RYAN

Gesture and attitude animate these partners in Peter Rose's Bird in Hand, *whose ceramic surface proves the drama and transformative process of extreme temperature from wood firing—and evokes bronze too. The bird perched on his shoulder is a convincing protector and totemic emblem.* —JB

Peter Rose

Bird in Hand | 2003

18 X 10 X 10 INCHES (45.7 X 25.4 X 25.4 CM)
Wheel-thrown clay; wood fired, cone 10

PHOTOS © GARY HEATHERLEY

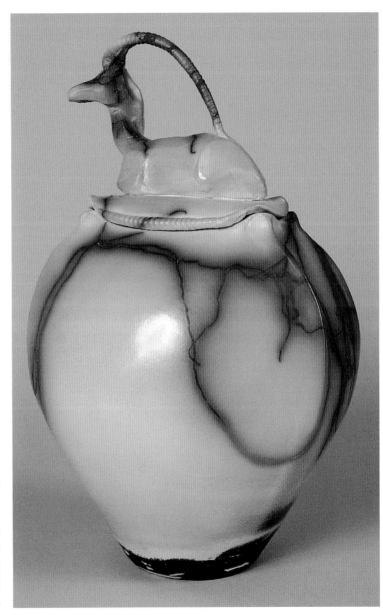

Susie Bogard

Gazelle | 2004

18 X 10 X 4½ INCHES (45.7 X 25.4 X 11.4 CM)

Thrown and hand-built stoneware;
terra sigillata; saggar fired with steel wool,
copper carbonate salt, and wood shavings;
raku fired, 1600°F (871°C)

PHOTO © ARTIST

Laura DeAngelis

Shannon | 2003

32 X 15 X 10 INCHES (81.3 X 38.1 X 25.4 CM)

Engobes, wood ash glaze, multi-fired, cone 04

PHOTO © E.G. SCHEMPF

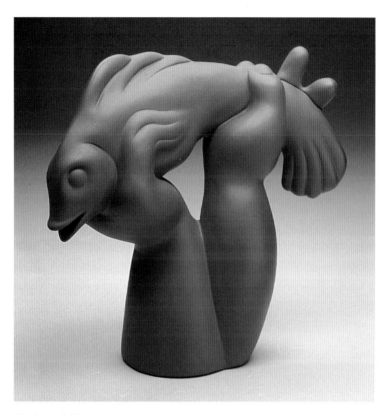

Richard Swanson

Proud Catch II Teapot | 2001

9¼ X 3½ X 9 INCHES (23.5 X 8.9 X 22.9 CM)

Cast and sanded fine-grained high-iron clay;
bisque fired, cone 06; fired until vitreous, cone 5

PHOTO © ARTIST

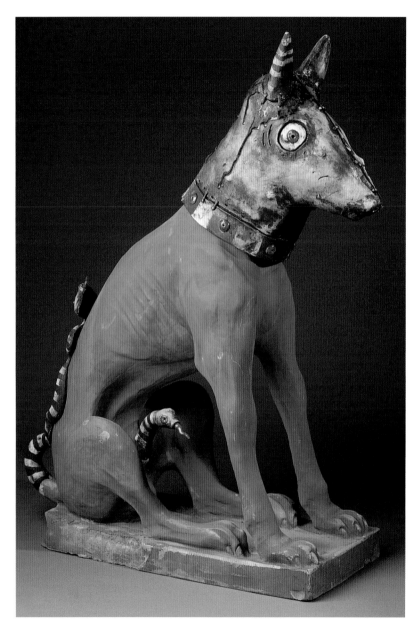

James Tisdale

Sparky—The Natural Sin | 2004

40 X 30 X 19 INCHES (101.6 X 76.2 X 48.3 CM)

Coil-built earthenware; electric fired, cone 03;
multi-fired glazes and underglazes

PHOTO © CHRIS ZALESKY

Karen Adelaar

La Petite | 2005

6½ X 6½ X 6 INCHES (16.5 X 16.5 X 15.2 CM)

Hand-built stoneware; wood fired, cone 10;
porcelain slips, nest wire, thread, weeds

PHOTO © JAMES DEE

The stand is constructed with wood and bicycle gears. The piece is kinetic and inspired by antique toys. —JT

James Tisdale

Monkey See (Kinetic) | 2004

42 X 24 X 24 INCHES (106.7 X 61 X 61 CM)

Coil-built earthenware; electric fired, cone 03; multi-fired glazes and underglazes; found objects

PHOTO © CHRIS ZALESKY

Carrianne Hendrickson

Dream of Backyard Dogs | 2004

16 X 9 X 11 INCHES (40.6 X 22.9 X 27.9 CM)
Hand-built and hollowed low-fire clay; electric fired,
cone 04; gouache, wax, low-fire glaze

PHOTOS © ARTIST

The painted imagery on the large eyes and beak surfaces are directly drawn from the work of Henri Rousseau. —EFK

Elizabeth F. Keller

The Dreamer's Tea | 2004

5¼ X 8½ X 4½ INCHES (13.3 X 21.6 X 11.4 CM)
Wheel-thrown, cut, and re-assembled porcelain;
electric fired, cone 5; slips, washes, glazes

PHOTOS © BILL EDMONDS

Kathleen Raven

Caravan Teapot #5, 25 Cent Show | 2005

12 X 7 X 16 INCHES (30.5 X 17.8 X 40.6 CM)

Altered slab red earthenware; electric fired,
cone 04; slips, engobes, underglazes, majolica

PHOTOS © BARBARA ZIMONICK

Laura DeAngelis

Twin Sisters | 2002

24 X 24 X 11 INCHES (61 X 61 X 27.9 CM)

Engobes, wood ash glaze, multi-fired, cone 04

PHOTO © MATTHEW MCFARLAND

Logan Wood gives us a work that strongly evokes dream and myth, status and aspiration, and the ambiguity of narrative and personal symbolism. Do raven-sized bluebirds equate feminine strength? Does light follows dark, or does dark lead to light? —JB

Logan Wood

Symbiosis | 2003

32 X 32 X 23 INCHES (81.3 X 81.3 X 58.4 CM)
Slab-built red clay; electric fired,
cone 6; engobe, glaze

PHOTO © BLACK CAT STUDIO

Kari K. Rives

Love Birds | 2005

9½ X 8 X 5¼ INCHES (24.1 X 20.3 X 13.3 CM)
Stoneware; gas fired, cone 10; oil pigments
PHOTO © ARTIST

My father's taxidermist/slaughter-house business—with its powerful images of hanging deer carcasses, piles of sawed-off animal feet, and freezers full of animal hides—was an overwhelming environment for me as a child. My artwork explores my father's traditions, unsettling subject matter, and lack of regard for life. —*LMP*

Lisa Merida-Paytes

Freezer Fish on Mica | 2005

18 X 24 X 19 INCHES (45.7 X 61 X 48.3 CM)
Coil-built stoneware; electric fired, cone 05; raku fired, cone 06
PHOTO © JAY BACHEMIN

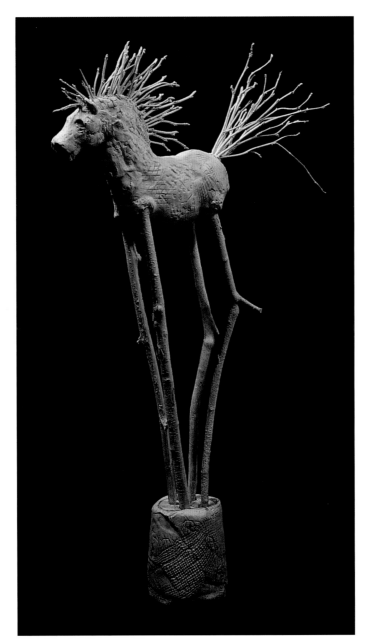

Anna Wiancko-Chasman

Stick Horse | 2004

42 X 18 X 12 INCHES (106.7 X 45.7 X 30.5 CM)

Slab-built clay with impressed texture; electric fired, cone 5; sticks, acrylic

PHOTO © KIRK JONASSON
COURTESY OF PORT ANGELES FINE ART CENTER

Laurie Sharkus

Wind Wolf | 2005

13 X 9 X 6 INCHES (33 X 22.9 X 15.2 CM)
Coil-built stoneware clay; electric
bisque fired, cone 07; smoke fired

PHOTO © ARTIST

Susanna Birley

Raku-Fired Polar Bear | 2005

8²/₃ X 16¹/₂ X 3¹⁵/₁₆ INCHES (22 X 42 X 10 CM)
Slab-built; electric fired, cone 06;
raku fired, cone 08

PHOTO © ARTIST

Tré Arenz

Wait–Watch | 1998

21 X 25 X 10 INCHES (53.3 X 63.5 X 25.4 CM)

Hand built; low-fire glaze

PHOTO © ESTATE OF THE ARTIST
COURTESY OF WILLIAM CAMPBELL CONTEMPORARY ART, INC.

Steve Irvine

Hydria Bestia | 2005

8¼ X 7⅞ X 5½ INCHES (21 X 20 X 14 CM)

Wheel-thrown and hand-built stoneware;
reduction fired, cone 10

PHOTOS © ARTIST

Peter Rose

Bird-Dog | 2003

12 X 8 X 15 INCHES (30.5 X 20.3 X 38.1 CM)

Wheel thrown, hand built; wood fired, cone 10

PHOTO © GARY HEATHERLEY

Linda Lighton

Seasnail | 2004

8 X 8 X 7½ INCHES (20.3 X 20.3 X 19.1 CM)

Thrown, coil-built, and slab-built whiteware; fired to various temperatures; glaze, cone 04; china paint, lusters

PHOTOS © E.G. SCHEMPF

The piece's power lies in the contrast between the sweet and horrific duality of life as Bitter Sweets happily chomps down another beautiful living creature. It is girly and charming, yet commanding at the same time. One is left to question why the remaining insects linger. —RB

Rebekah Bogard

Bitter Sweets | 2005

31 X 34 X 23 INCHES (78.7 X 86.4 X 58.4 CM)
Slab-built and slip-cast earthenware;
electric fired, cone 04; oil paint, metal rod
PHOTOS © ARTIST

173

Shari McWilliams

HYPP: Horse Disease Series | 2005

17½ X 6 X 18 INCHES (44.5 X 15.2 X 45.7 CM)

Slab-built stoneware; gas fired in reduction,
cone 6; engobes

PHOTO © ARTIST

Irianna Kanellopoulou

60 Minutes of Happiness | 2005

3⅓ X 3⅛ X 1¾ INCHES (8.5 X 8 X 4.5 CM)

Hand-built and slip-cast earthenware;
electric fired, cone 04

PHOTO © ANDREW BARCHAM

Classic Rodin-like modeling expresses the empathy that is Beth Cavener Stichter's forte. Here, her goats seem to ripple with energy, the natural consequence of vigorous and convincing modeling. —JB

Beth Cavener Stichter

The Inquisitors | 2004

65 X 80 X 28 INCHES (165.1 X 203.2 X 71.1 CM)

Stoneware; bisque fired, cone 08; porcelain slip, cone 6

PHOTO © ARTIST
COURTESY OF GARTH CLARK GALLERY AND MARK DEL VECCHIO

Kenneth Ferguson

Bull on Bronze Cart | 2004

14 X 25 X 10 INCHES (35.6 X 63.5 X 25.4 CM)

Black stoneware; bronze

PHOTO COURTESY OF GARTH CLARK GALLERY, NY

Reynold Ho

Earth, Wind, and Fire | 2000

17 X 20 X 12 INCHES (43.2 X 50.8 X 30.5 CM)

Slab-built ceramic; electric fired, cone 5

PHOTO © MING TSHING

Annemie Heylen has done not too much—just enough; it's like the I Ching cast described as "the most perfect grace." —JB

Annemie Heylen

Rejection | 2005

10¼ X 5½ X 5½ INCHES (26 X 14 X 14 CM)

Coil-built stoneware; electric fired, 1832°F (1000°C); terra sigillata, 2192°F (1200°C)

PHOTO © JANNIEK HELDER

Heather Murray

Curious Rabbit | 2005

7¾ X 6½ X 6 INCHES (19.7 X 16.5 X 15.2 CM)

Thrown and assembled stoneware;
electric fired, cone 6; stain

PHOTO © ARTIST

Terry Ann Ostovar

Reflection–Ptarmigan | 2005

8½ X 8 X 4 INCHES (21.6 X 20.3 X 10.2 CM)

Slumped, paddled, textured, pinched, and slab-formed clay; electric fired, cone 04; burnished, terra sigillata, glaze

PHOTO © PAYAM OSTOVAR

The spirit of Brancusi lives in Norman D. Holen's fishy sculpture. It's easy to imagine that this finless swimmer might be trapped in a glaze of seaweed netting. —JB

Norman D. Holen

Fish No. 6 (Glazed) | 1972

12¾ X 14⅜ X 6½ INCHES (32.4 X 36.5 X 16.5 CM)

Press-molded earthenware; electric fired, cone 4

PHOTO © PETER LEE

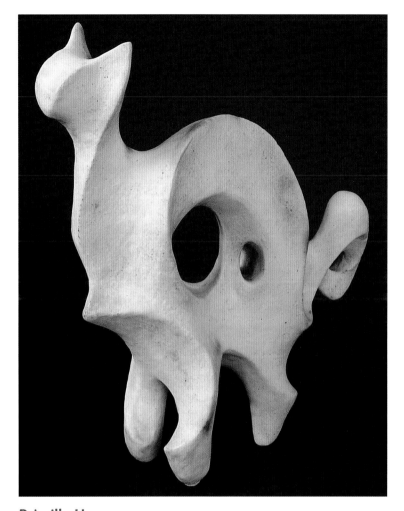

Priscilla Heep

What's for Dinner? | 2005

16 X 13 X 5 INCHES (40.6 X 33 X 12.7 CM)

Slab-built and coil-built stoneware;
electric fired, cone 6; glazes, multi-fired

PHOTO © SARAH S. LEWIS

Marie-Elena Ottman

Quarrelers/Peleones | 2004

19 X 25 X 13 INCHES (48.3 X 63.5 X 33 CM)

Coil-built earthenware; electric fired,
cone 03; slips, underglazes, sgraffito

PHOTO © GEOFFREY CARR PHOTOGRAPHY

Jenna Perstlinger

Year of the Monkey | 2004

20½ X 14½ X 2¾ INCHES (52.1 X 36.8 X 7 CM)

Hollow slip-cast earthenware; electric fired,
cone 04; commercial glaze, cone 06

PHOTO © RIC HELSTROM

Jack Thompson, AKA Jugo de Vegetales

Animus Conveyance | 2002

12 X 11 X 19 INCHES (30.5 X 27.9 X 48.3 CM)

Cast and modeled paper clay; electric fired, cone 05;
bronze powders, graphite, alkyd medium

PHOTO © JOHN CARLANO

Etta Winigrad

Puppet | 2001

16 X 24 X 8 INCHES (40.6 X 61 X 20.3 CM)
Hand-built low-fire white talc; electric fired,
cone 02; smoked
PHOTO © ARTIST

Clay serves all honest visions and Elizabeth Zacher's is freshly personal. Perhaps the artist is imagining the future of genetic experimentation? —JB

Elizabeth Zacher

Pasteurella | 2004

17 X 8 X 13 INCHES (43.2 X 20.3 X 33 CM)
Ceramic; acrylics, rabbit fur, rabbit foot

PHOTO © ARTIST

Brian McArthur

Goose Boy | 2005

29 X 12 X 29 INCHES (73.7 X 30.5 X 73.7 CM)

Slab-modeled paper clay; reduction fired, cone 6

PHOTO © ARTIST

The sum of Cheryl Tall's usual obsessive, signature pinching is here in her Blind Choice. *This cluster of figures creates drama and suspicion: Is that someone in a cat suit, or does the cat have human gloves on?* —JB

Cheryl Tall

Blind Choice | 2001–2005

27 X 15 X 15 INCHES (68.6 X 38.1 X 38.1 CM)

Coil-built architectural clay; electric fired, cone 04; slip, oxides, glaze, terra sigillata

PHOTO © BRUCE TALL

Janis Mars Wunderlich

Jumping over Her Head | 2002

14 X 8 X 6 INCHES (35.6 X 20.3 X 15.2 CM)

Hand-built earthenware; cone 3; slip, underglaze, overglaze, cone 04

PHOTOS © ARTIST

Nina G. Koepcke

Tales of Krylou: The Animal Quartet | 1994

22 X 16 X 12 INCHES (55.9 X 40.6 X 30.5 CM)

Coil-built sculpture-mix clay; electric fired,
cone 02; multi-fired, underglaze, glaze

*I use dogs as
protagonists
because they have
completely integrated
themselves into the
human world of gestured
poses of affection. In
this way, they partici-
pate fully in their
humans' lives. —AR*

Ann Roberts
The Last Waltz | 2004

15⅜ X 9⁷⁄₁₆ X 7¹⁄₁₆ INCHES (39 X 24 X 18 CM)
Hollow hand-built white earthenware; soluble
mineral salts; electric fired, cone 02

PHOTO © ARTIST

Katy Rush

Feline Masquerade Teapot | 2005

10 X 6 X 5 INCHES (25.4 X 15.2 X 12.7 CM)

Hand-built porcelain; electric fired, cone 6

PHOTO © DANIEL BARKER
COURTESY OF FERRIN GALLERY

Laszlo Fekete

Wild Horses Urn | 2004

22 X 27 INCHES (55.9 X 68.6 CM)

Porcelain

PHOTO COURTESY OF GARTH CLARK GALLERY, NY

Karl Kuhns

Debra Parker-Kuhns

Running Dogs Pot | 2004

8 X 6 X 6 INCHES (20.3 X 15.2 X 15.2 CM)

Wheel-thrown and hand-built porcelain; electric
fired, cone 8; polychrome slips, clear glaze

PHOTO © ARTISTS

David Regan accomplishes an exquisite ceramic assemblage, an apocalyptic
Noah's Ark, in which the animals may be repeating our folly. —JB

David Regan

Ark | 2003

22 X 28 X 16 INCHES (55.9 X 71.1 X 40.6 CM)

Porcelain

PHOTO COURTESY OF GARTH CLARK GALLERY, NY

Sarah K. Whitlock

Absurd Bird #10 | 2004

7 X 5½ X 5 INCHES (17.8 X 14 X 12.7 CM)

Thrown, altered, and slip-cast stoneware;
electric fired, cone 6

PHOTO © ARTIST

Logan Wood

Corridor | 2003

23 X 25 X 8 INCHES (58.4 X 63.5 X 20.3 CM)
Slab-built red clay; cone 6; glaze
PHOTO © BLACK CAT STUDIO

Adelaide Paul

Neutered | 2005

12 X 21 INCHES (30.5 X 53.3 CM)
Porcelain; mixed media
PHOTO COURTESY OF GARTH CLARK GALLERY, NY

Kisses Number 2 explores the idea of cuteness and innocence juxtaposed with sexual curiosity. The concepts of "cute" and "girly," and their exclusion from the serious art world, are topics I am profoundly interested in. —RB

Rebekah Bogard

Kisses Number 2 | 2005

31 X 30 X 24 INCHES (78.7 X 76.2 X 61 CM)

Slab-built and slip-cast earthenware; electric fired, cone 04; underglaze, glaze, cone 04; metal rod

PHOTOS © ARTIST

Asia Mathis

Cat in Plow Pose | 2003

15 X 16 X 9 INCHES (38.1 X 40.6 X 22.9 CM)

Slab-built porcelain; electric fired, cone 6

PHOTO © MICHAEL COTHRAN

Nan Jacobsohn

Sgrafitto Cat | 2003

18 X 15 X 9 INCHES (45.7 X 38.1 X 22.9 CM)

Coil-built stoneware; sgrafitto through black slip;
electric fired, cone 6

PHOTO © JOHN CUMMINGS

Patrick L. Dougherty

Spanish Moon | 2005

4 X 25 INCHES (10.2 X 63.5 CM)

Wheel-thrown white earthenware; electric fired,
cone 04; underglazes, clear glaze

PHOTO © GREG KUCHIK

Linda Cordell transposes Giacomo Balla's Dynamism of a Dog on a Leash, *1912, to her fully dimensional— and operational— running cock.* —JB

Linda Cordell

running cock | 2005

22 X 16 X 7 INCHES (55.9 X 40.6 X 17.8 CM)

Slip-cast and hand-built porcelain; reduction fired, cone 10; found metal turntable

PHOTO © ARTIST

Marta Matray Gloviczki

Mikhail | 2003

9 X 12 X 1 INCHES (22.9 X 30.5 X 2.5 CM)

Hand-built porcelain; cone 6

PHOTO © PETER LEE

Isabel Mikell

Horse Vase | 2005

12 X 3 X 5 INCHES (30.5 X 7.6 X 12.7 CM)
Slab-built porcelain; reduction fired,
cone 10; underglaze
PHOTO © GUY NICHOL

Peggy Peak

Horse in the Mist | 2004

DIAMETER, 12 INCHES (30.5 CM)
Wheel-thrown porcelain clay; raku glaze
PHOTO © ARTIST

Laurie Shaman

Wall Plate: Dog Days | 2005

DIAMETER, 13 ½ INCHES (34.3 CM)

Slab-built earthenware; electric fired,
cone 04; underglaze, glaze, cone 06

PHOTO © PETER KIAR

Jeri Hollister

4 Horses, Persian Drawing, 02–36 | 2002

48 X 64 X 2 INCHES (121.9 X 162.6 X 5.1 CM)

Slab-built and extruded earthenware;
electric fired, cone 03; slip, wash, glaze

PHOTO © ARTIST

A spectrum of critters, free at last, seems frozen in a moment of indecision—scatter, escape, or stay together? Wendy Walgate's savvy use of mold-made found ceramic forms and a keen sense of color composition, symbolism, and meaning pervades her work. —JB

Wendy Walgate

My Little Chair | 2005

24 X 11 X 10 INCHES (61 X 27.9 X 25.4 CM)

Slip-cast white earthenware; glaze, cone 06; vintage child's chair

PHOTOS © ARTIST

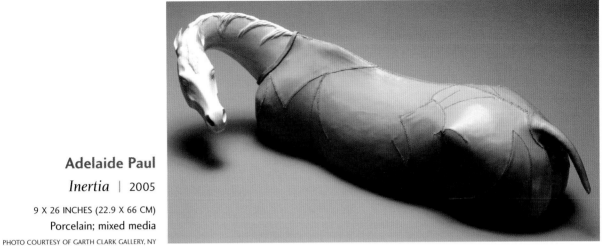

Adelaide Paul

Inertia | 2005

9 X 26 INCHES (22.9 X 66 CM)
Porcelain; mixed media
PHOTO COURTESY OF GARTH CLARK GALLERY, NY

Linda Cordell

squirrel bomb | 2005

15 X 9 X 9 INCHES (38.1 X 22.9 X 22.9 CM)
Slip-cast and hand-built porcelain; reduction
fired, cone 10; resin-coated base
PHOTO © ARTIST

Novie Trump

Blackbird | 2005

3 X 8 X 3 INCHES (7.6 X 20.3 X 7.6 CM)
Hand-built raku clay; raku fired
PHOTO © GREG STALEY

Yoona Welling

Tasmanian Devil | 1991–2005

2 X 1 9/16 X 3 15/16 INCHES (5 X 4 X 10 CM)
Slip-cast stoneware; electric fired,
cone 8; raw fired, wax resist
PHOTO © UFFE SCHULZE

*Wondering what goes on in the animal mind and body
has been a driving force in my exploration of the
confluence of form and motion that animal bodies imply.* —EW

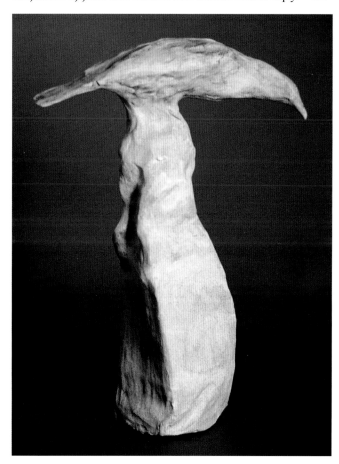

Elizabeth Waite

Pestilence Is in the Eye of the Beholder | 2005

17½ X 12½ X 7 INCHES (44.5 X 31.8 X 17.8 CM)
Hand-built stoneware; electric fired,
2134°F (1168°C); oxides, underglaze

Ron Meyers

Tea Bowl | 2005

3½ X 5½ INCHES (8.9 X 14 CM)
Wheel-thrown stoneware;
wood fired, cone 10
PHOTO © W. MONTGOMERY

Cynthia Bringle

Untitled | 2005

33 X 14 INCHES (83.8 X 35.6 CM)
Thrown and altered; wood fired, cone 9
PHOTO © TOM MILLS

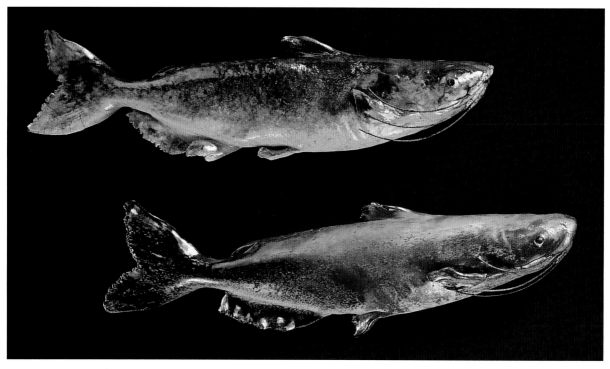

Megan R. Wright

Catfish | 2005

EACH, 4½ X 16½ X 2 INCHES (11.4 X 16.5 X 5.1 CM)
Slab-built and press-molded raku; gas fired
in reduction, 1800°F (982°C); raku fired

PHOTO © WILBUR MONTGOMERY

Wesley L. Smith

Creeper | 2000

4 X 6 X 6 INCHES (10.2 X 15.2 X 15.2 CM)
Pinched and coil-built white stoneware;
electric fired, cone 04; glaze,
enamel paint, synthetic hair

PHOTO © ARTIST

Laurie Sharkus

Nomad | 2005

4 X 19 X 16 INCHES (10.2 X 48.3 X 40.6 CM)
Slab- and coil-built stoneware clay; electric
fired, cone 04; painted, smoke fired

PHOTOS © ARTIST

Jenny Mendes

Ike | 2004

6 X 7 X 4 INCHES (15.2 X 17.8 X 10.2 CM)
Coil built; electric fired,
cone 03; terra sigillata

PHOTO © HEATHER PROTZ

Caroline Douglas

Rabbit Teapot | 2005

9 X 4½ X 3 INCHES (22.9 X 11.4 X 7.6 CM)
Hand-built stoneware; reduction fired,
cone 4; slips, glazes, underglaze pencil

PHOTO © KEN SANVILLE

Angel Olegario Luna

Monkey Dreamer: Arbol 'n' Food | 2005

20 X 6 X 6 INCHES (50.8 X 15.2 X 15.2 CM)

Thrown, altered, and hand-built stoneware; fired in
reduction, cone 10; vitreous slip glaze

PHOTOS © ARTIST

Susanna Birley

Raku-Fired Goose | 2005

15¾ X 13⅜ X 5⅞ INCHES (40 X 34 X 15 CM)

Press-molded and coiled paper clay; electric fired,
cone 06; raku fired, cone 08

PHOTO © ARTIST

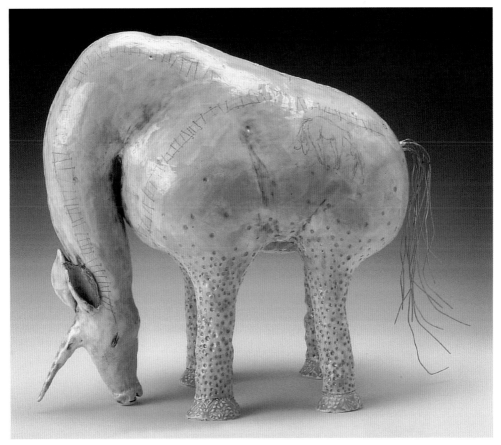

Asia Mathis

Unicorn in Forward Fold | 2005

20 X 21 X 10 INCHES (50.8 X 53.3 X 25.4 CM)
Slab-built porcelain; electric fired, cone 6
PHOTO © MICHAEL COTHRAN

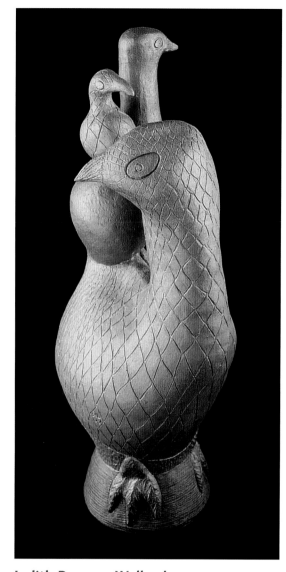

These birds, perched one atop the other, are totally grounded in the clay of which they are made—no wings, no tails. The top bird is on a dowel so that the direction of his gaze can be rotated a full 360°. —JRW

Judith Romney Wolbach

Sentries | 2004

23½ X 10 X 8 INCHES (59.7 X 25.4 X 20.3 CM)
Coil-built and pinched black and red clays;
gas fired, cone 10; incised, oxides

PHOTO © JAN STEVENSON

Howard Gerstein

Bird Menorah | 2004

5½ X 12¼ X 4⅝ INCHES (14 X 31.1 X 11.8 CM)

Slab-built terra cotta; electric fired, cone 04;
unglazed, fumed

PHOTO © MONICA RIPLEY

Etta Winigrad

Under My Wing | 1997

25¼ X 16 X 11 INCHES (64.1 X 40.6 X 27.9 CM)
Hand-built low-fire white talc body;
electric fired, cone 02; smoked
PHOTO © ARTIST

Pamela H. Brewer

Yin and Yang | 2005

LEFT, 11 ½ X 9 X 8 INCHES (29.2 X 22.9 X 20.3 CM);
RIGHT, 14 ½ X 12 X 8 INCHES (36.8 X 30.5 X 20.3 CM)

Coil-built red earthenware; terra
sigillata; electric fired, cone 04;
twice fired with oxide stains

PHOTO © TIM BARNWELL

Ann Mortimer, C.M.

Bird Forms | 1980–2005

5 ½ X 7 X 4 ¾ INCHES (14 X 18 X 12 CM)
White clay; electric fired, cone 6, cone 9;
sprayed and poured glazes

PHOTO © MARK EVESON

Marabou storks feed off rubbish dumps in Africa. They are carrion eaters, so the title is a tongue-in-cheek bit of humor. —AM

Ann Marais

In Search of Gastronomic Adventure | 2004

2¾ X 9¹/₁₆ X 11 INCHES (7 X 23 X 28 CM)
Slab-built and drape-molded porcelain; electric fired, cone 6; underglaze stain, clear glaze
PHOTO © ARTIST

Frank A. Gosar

Fairy Tern | 2002

6 X 9 INCHES (15.2 X 22.9 CM)
Reduction fired, cone 10; overglaze, oxides, stains
PHOTO © JON MEYERS

Kevin B. Hardin

Bird Woman | 2004

5 X 3½ X 8½ INCHES (12.7 X 8.9 X 21.6 CM)

Hand-built stoneware; electric fired, cone 6;
painted patina, wood

PHOTO © DON WHEELER

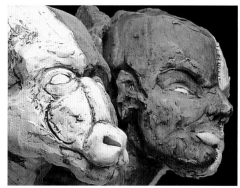

Liza Domeier

Self Portrait #2 | 2003

23 X 14 X 12 INCHES (58.4 X 35.6 X 30.5 CM)

Slab-built and pinched mid-range stoneware;
electric fired, cone 2; slips, stains

PHOTOS © ARTIST

Lisa Clague

Convoluted Dream | 2000

80 X 48 X 16 INCHES (203.2 X 121.9 X 40.6 CM)
Coil built; metal, glazes, stains, wax, cone 04
PHOTOS © TOM MILLS

Pavel G. Amromin

Toy Soldier II | 2005

7½ X 3 X 3 INCHES (19.1 X 7.6 X 7.6 CM)

Hand-built terra cotta; electric fired,
cone 04; enamel paint, wood

PHOTO © TAMMY MARINUZZI

Roxanne Jackson

Virtue | 2004

52 X 11 ½ X 11 INCHES (132.1 X 29.2 X 27.9 CM)

Coil-built terra cotta; electric fired, cone 04; low-fire slips, glazes, flocking

PHOTOS © LARRY GAWEL

Debra Evelyn Sloan

Welcome Mat | 2004

21 X 24 X 12 INCHES (53.3 X 61 X 30.5 CM)

Hollow slab-built red earthenware; electric fired,
cone 01; slips, paint, stones, thermoplastic

PHOTO © KENJI NAGAI

Kerry Jameson

Two Sitting Bulldogs | 2002

14⅛ X 9¹/₁₆ X 9⁷/₁₆ INCHES (36 X 23 X 24 CM)

Coil-built grogged buff; electric fired, 1100°F (593°C);
slips, glaze, 1060°F (571°C)

PHOTO © HOWIE

Debbie Fong

Sox | 2005

5 X 2¾ X 7 INCHES (12.7 X 7 X 17.8 CM)
Wheel-thrown, altered and assembled; pit fired

PHOTO © SAADI SHAPIRO AND DAR FONG

Daphne Gillen

Tattoo (Teapot) | 2005

12 X 4 X 8 INCHES (30.5 X 10.2 X 20.3 CM)

Hand-built stoneware with porcelain slip; electric fired, cone 01; hand-drawn graffiti, cone 05

PHOTO © TOM LIDEN

Ten clay inserts of the same size were incorporated into railings for the 22nd Street Bayonne Station. Each relates a historic fact about the town. The caption under the pigeon reads: "I Dreamt I Went to War in my Maidenform Pigeon Vest." —ST

Susan Tunick

PIGEON VEST by Maidenform
[Bayonne, NJ, Light Rail Station] | 2003

20 X 17½ X 1¼ INCHES (50.8 X 44.5 X 3.2 CM)
Slab-built, hand-carved, and impressed bisque ware;
electric fired, cone 3; glaze, cone 04
PHOTO © PETER MAUSS/ESTO

Sandra L. Lance

Loon's Summer Plumage | 2005

3 X 13 X 13 INCHES (7.6 X 33 X 33 CM)

Wheel-thrown and altered porcelain;
electric fired, cone 06; sgraffito, slips

PHOTO © ARTIST

Peggy Peak

Zebra | 2005

DIAMETER, 12 INCHES (30.5 CM)

Wheel-thrown porcelain clay;
raku glaze, gold leaf

PHOTO © ARTIST

James Tingey

Desert Raccoon | 2004

9 X 8 X 8 INCHES (22.9 X 20.3 X 20.3 CM)

Wheel-thrown porcelain; natural gas fired,
cone 10; sgraffito

PHOTO © ARTIST

Unlike painting's function as a "window," pottery's concrete, dimensional space lures the viewer to observe what is at once real and pictorial. Tim Christensen-Kirby's vessel might owe a debt to the fabled Minoan octopus pot. —JB

Tim Christensen-Kirby

Squids and Gannets | 2005

13 X 14 X 14 INCHES (33 X 35.6 X 35.6 CM)
Wheel-thrown porcelain; propane fired,
cone 7; oxides, sgraffito

PHOTO © ARTIST

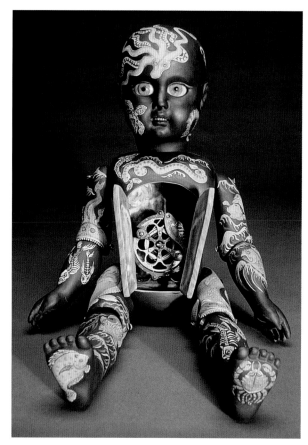

The teeming sea animals covering this human figure represent the inner reality of the unconscious mind. Each animal is a dream message to be "caught" as the dreamer traverses the night sea. —MW

Maryann Webster
Night Sea | 2005

14 X 13 X 14 INCHES (35.6 X 33 X 35.6 CM)
Slip-cast porcelain; electric fired, painted engobes,
cone 5; antique glass eyes, reel, lure

PHOTOS © ARTIST

What dreams invade Jungian turf? Jim Budde's Wakeful Intent *poses challenging questions. This ape's dynamic posturing contrasts with the repose of his dream-creator, and stylized modeling and surface texture empha-size the unreality of their world.* —JB

Jim Budde

Wakeful Intent | 2002

34 X 25 X 12 INCHES (86.4 X 63.5 X 30.5 CM)
Slab-built stoneware; electric fired,
cone 3; glaze, cone 08

PHOTO © ARTIST
COLLECTION OF DAVID BANKS

Wendy Walgate

Red Is Ambition | 2005

14 X 10 X 8 INCHES (35.6 X 25.4 X 20.3 CM)

Slip-cast white earthenware; glaze, cone 06;
vintage ceramic container, marble

PHOTO © ARTIST

Skuja Braden

Chick | 2004

16 X 10 X 8 INCHES (40.6 X 25.4 X 20.3 CM)

Hand-built porcelain; electric fired,
cone 6; inscribed designs, glazes

PHOTOS © TONY NOVELOVO
COURTESY OF JOHN NATSOULAS GALLERY

This doggie-encrusted Fido by Mary Engel is a playful and humorous visual double-entendre. Its busy and rich accreted surface is a feast for the eyes. —JB

Mary Engel

Fido | 2004

18 X 17 X 7 INCHES (45.7 X 43.2 X 17.8 CM)

Clay

PHOTO © WALKER MONTGOMERY

Gary Dinnen

Critters in a Bowl 2 | 2005

30 X 24 X 30 INCHES (76.2 X 61 X 76.2 CM)

Slab-built raku sculpture mix; electric fired, cone 06

PHOTO © CARI LAZANSKY

Marie-Elena Ottman

Chameleon | 2004

22 X 16 X 23 INCHES (55.9 X 40.6 X 58.4 CM)

Coil-built earthenware; electric fired, cone 03; slips, underglazes, sgraffito

PHOTOS © GEOFFREY CARR PHOTOGRAPHY

Tré Arenz

Comfort–Flock | 1995

20 X 28 X 21 INCHES (50.8 X 71.1 X 53.3 CM)

Commercially-cast vitreous china

This piece was inspired by a Tibetan chant that compares samsara—*the trials and tribulations of everyday life—with the image of bees going 'round and 'round in a jar.* —CS

Cynthia Siegel

Samsara | 2003

17 X 35 X 27 INCHES (43.2 X 88.9 X 68.6 CM)

Thrown, altered, and press-molded terra cotta; cone 02; underglaze, cone 05; glass, recycled asphalt

PHOTOS © STAN EINHORN AND ARTIST

Pavel G. Amromin

Toy Soldier I | 2005

11 X 5½ X 5½ INCHES (27.9 X 14 X 14 CM)

Hand-built terra cotta; electric fired, cone 04; enamel paint, wood, glass

PHOTO © TAMMY MARINUZZI

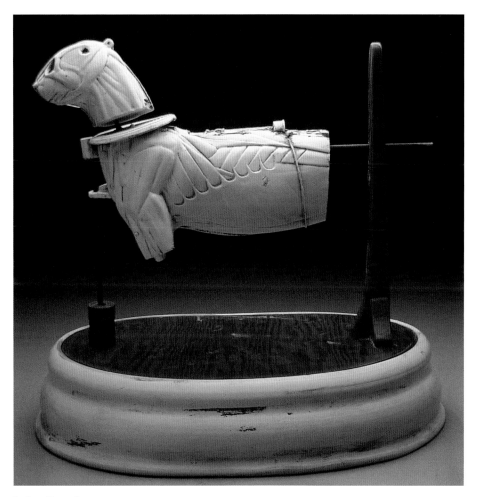

John Byrd

Untitled Cat Piece | 2002

15 X 15 INCHES (38.1 X 38.1 CM)
Mixed media
PHOTO COURTESY OF GARTH CLARK GALLERY, NY

Red Weldon Sandlin

Spoutings of a Cateapillar | 2004

18¾ X 9¼ X 9 INCHES (47.6 X 23.5 X 22.9 CM)

Coil- and slab-built white earthenware; electric fired,
cone 04; hand painted underglaze, oxide, cone 06

PHOTOS © CHARLEY AKERS
COURTESY OF FERRIN GALLERY

With ears like
weapons and fur
like chain mail, Rytas
Jakimavicius's lagomorph
is ready for serious com-
petition in some mythic
gladiatorial game. —JB

Rytas Jakimavičius
Playing Rabbit | 2002

14³⁄₁₆ X 6¹¹⁄₁₆ X 9¹³⁄₁₆ INCHES (36 X 17 X 25 CM)
Hand-built porcelain; electric fired, cone 6

PHOTO © ARTIST

Timeless friends are appropriately portrayed by Frances Norton's casual—even naïve—modeling, which contributes to the charm of the piece. —JB

Frances Norton

I'm Not for Tea | 1998

7 1/16 X 5 1/2 X 5 1/2 INCHES (18 X 14 X 14 CM)
Hand-built and cast stoneware, slip, and paper clay; gas fired in reduction; wire armature, oxides, clear glaze

PHOTOS © ARTIST

Amy Goldstein-Rice

Likin' Milk | 2004

15 X 7 X 9 INCHES (38.1 X 17.8 X 22.9 CM)

Wheel-thrown and hand-built
white earthenware; electric fired,
cone 02; engobes, underglaze,
crawl glaze, plastic eyes

PHOTO © MARK OLENCKI

Kate Fisher

The Coy and a Peach | 2005

9 X 5 X 5 INCHES (22.9 X 12.7 X 12.7 CM)

Wheel-thrown porcelain; oxidation fired,
cone 6; decals, cone 017

PHOTO © STEVE SCHNIEDER

Salinda Dahl

The Flower | 2004

20 X 15 X 9 INCHES (50.8 X 38.1 X 22.9 CM)
Slab-built earthenware; gas fired;
stain, glaze, oil
PHOTOS © SETH TICE-LEWIS

Elizabeth Coleman

Flight | 2002

EACH, 5 X 2½ X 4 INCHES (12.7 X 6.4 X 10.2 CM)
Press-molded porcelain; electric fired,
cone 6; embedded glass, glaze, stains
PHOTO © BRYAN HEATON

Kurt Weiser

Masquerade | 2002

13 X 14 INCHES (33 X 35.6 CM)
Porcelain
PHOTO © CRAIG SMITH
COURTESY OF GARTH CLARK GALLERY, NY

Jenny Lind's Ms. Chita and Friend *reveals her talent as painter and colorist. Her intuitive approach to imagery results in romantic and spiritual juxtapositions of subjects.* —JB

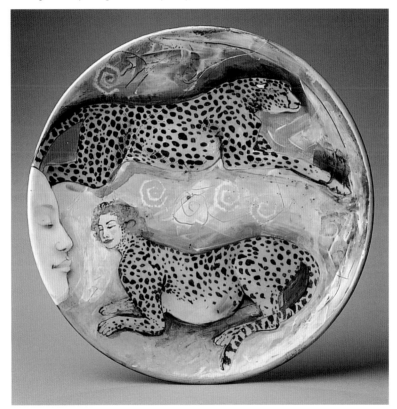

Jenny Lind

Ms. Chita and Friend | 2003

16 X 2¼ INCHES (40.6 X 5.7 CM)
Thrown earthenware; electric fired,
cone 03; underglaze, clear glaze

PHOTO © WENDY MCEAHERN

Jean-Pierre Larocque

Untitled Horse | 2000

29 X 29 X 12 INCHES (73.7 X 73.7 X 30.5 CM)

Stoneware

PHOTO COURTESY OF GARTH CLARK GALLERY, NY

Anne L. Rafferty

Romagnola Calf | 2004

13½ X 20 X 6 INCHES (34.3 X 50.8 X 15.2 CM)

Pinched stoneware; anagama wood fired
with flash slip, cone 12

PHOTO © WALKER MONTGOMERY

Pamela Earnshaw Kelly

Red Arrow | 2003

9 X 16 X 9 INCHES (22.9 X 40.6 X 22.9 CM)
Slab-built raku clay; raku fired, cone 05;
lithium rutile slip, paint

Beth Cavener Stichter

The Secret Keeper | 2003

9 X 10 X 9 INCHES (22.9 X 25.4 X 22.9 CM)

Porcelain, Mason stain

PHOTO © ARTIST

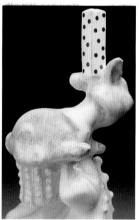

Elissa Armstrong

Circles, Rectangles | 2003

8 X 5 X 3 INCHES (20.3 X 12.7 X 7.6 CM)
Hand-built earthenware; electric fired,
cone 04; decals, cone 018

PHOTOS © ARTIST

Amy M. Santoferraro

Bathroom Cup | 2004

5 X 4 X 3 INCHES (12.7 X 10.2 X 7.6 CM)

Slip-cast porcelain; electric fired, cone 6

PHOTO © ARTIST

Amy M. Santoferraro

Road Show Prop #SRJ93572 | 2004

4 X 6 X 3 INCHES (10.2 X 15.2 X 7.6 CM)

Slip-cast porcelain; electric fired, cone 6;
decals, luster, cone 018

PHOTO © ARTIST

Renee Audette

Bunny Snowglobe | 2004

7 X 4 X 4 INCHES (17.8 X 10.2 X 10.2 CM)
Slip-cast porcelain; electric fired, cone 6;
cast in resin; slips, glazes, gold leaf

PHOTO © JOHN KNAUB

Kathleen Laurie

Blue Rabbit Jar | 2000

5 X 4 X 3 INCHES (12.7 X 10.2 X 7.6 CM)
Thrown and altered earthenware;
electric fired, cone 04; terra sigillata

PHOTO © ARTIST

Family Diary's *imagery elicits a contemplation of mortality and legacy. The symbol of book, explicated by the title but then obscured by mysterious animal imagery, nevertheless implies a continuity of spirit. The richness of porcelain contributes materially to its meaning.* —JB

Chuck McWeeny

Family Diary | 1994

8½ X 11 X 14 INCHES (21.6 X 27.9 X 35.6 CM)
Slip-cast porcelain; soda fired, cone 10

PHOTOS © ARTIST

Shari McWilliams

Strangles | 2005

10 X 11 X 15 INCHES (25.4 X 27.9 X 38.1 CM)

Hand-built stoneware; gas fired
in reduction, cone 6; engobes

PHOTO © ARTIST

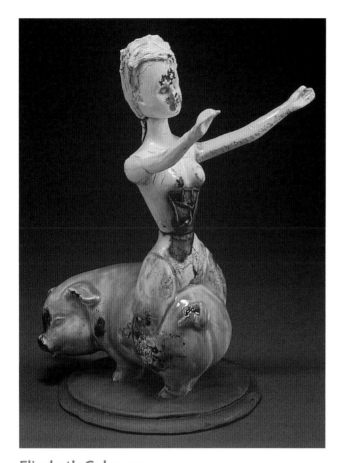

Elizabeth Coleman

Pork Princess | 2003

12 X 6 X 3 INCHES (30.5 X 15.2 X 7.6 CM)

Press-molded porcelain; electric fired, cone 6; embedded glass, glaze, stains, cast lead crystal, oil paint

PHOTO © BRYAN HEATON

Katy Rush

Pet Dishgirl | 2003

10 X 5 X 3 INCHES (25.4 X 12.7 X 7.6 CM)

Slip-cast porcelain; electric fired, cone 6

PHOTO © ARTIST
COURTESY OF FERRIN GALLERY

Genya Glass

Icarus | 2005

11 X 12 X 7 INCHES (27.9 X 30.5 X 17.8 CM)
Hand-built earthenware; electric fired,
cone 06; pigments
PHOTO © ERIC NORBOM

Beth Cavener Stichter

Cornered Hare | 2003

22 X 37 X 33 INCHES (55.9 X 94 X 83.8 CM)

Stoneware

PHOTO © ARTIST

Susan Halls

A Sort of Wild Pig | 2004

7½ X 13 X 3¹⁵⁄₁₆ INCHES (19 X 33 X 10 CM)

Thrown and assembled paper clay; raku fired, smoked, cone 07; slip, metal

PHOTO © PATRICK VINGO

Elaine Bolz

Iguana Column | 2003

26 X 12 X 10 INCHES (66 X 30.5 X 25.4 CM)

Slab-built and sculpted white earthenware; electric fired, cone 02; airbrushed underglaze, glaze, cone 05

PHOTO © MARGO GEIST

I attempt to expose the unseen core, the essential structure of skeletal or embryonic animal references. I find these references provocative and they offer me an opportunity to understand our own growth and decay. —*LMP*

Lisa Merida-Paytes

Frozen Fish on Granite | 2005

30 X 24 X 33 INCHES (76.2 X 61 X 83.8 CM)

Coil-built stoneware; electric fired, cone 05; raku fired, cone 06

PHOTO © JAY BACHEMIN

Red Weldon Sandlin

A Little Lesson in Gravitea | 2005

12 X 15 X 12 INCHES (30.5 X 38.1 X 30.5 CM)

Slab- and coil-built earthenware; electric fired, cone 04; hand painted underglaze, iron oxide, low-fire glaze, cone 06

PHOTOS © CHARLEY AKERS
COURTESY OF FERRIN GALLERY

Daphne Gillen

Boar Chowing Down | 1999

20 X 16 X 14 INCHES (50.8 X 40.6 X 35.6 CM)

Hand-built stoneware; electric fired,
cone 01; raku fired, cone 05

PHOTO © TOM LIDEN

The black dog represents the id: it wants what it wants. —JC

Jennie Chien

Black Dog #5, Scratching | 2000

13 X 8½ X 12 INCHES (33 X 21.6 X 30.5 CM)

Slab- and coil-built stoneware; electric fired, cone 6; slips, sgraffito, copper-coated after firing with copper powder suspended in shellac

PHOTO © ARTIST

Debra Evelyn Sloan

Green Pastures | 2004

17 X 21 X 11 INCHES (43.2 X 53.3 X 27.9 CM)

Hollow slab-built red earthenware; electric fired,
cone 01; slips, paint, flocked wood

PHOTO © KENJI NAGAI

This austere old bird sits on his perch like his archaic precursors, the Stylites (Christian ascetics who sat atop columns to prove their faith.) Judith Romney Wolbach has moodily interpreted the spirit of these lonely first-century believers. —JB

Judith Romney Wolbach
Stylite | 2005

23 X 8 X 8 INCHES (58.4 X 20.3 X 20.3 CM)
Coil-built and pinched red clay; gas fired, cone 10; incised, oxides

PHOTO © JAN STEVENSON

Ron Mazanowski

Rhino Pot | 1991

38 X 18 INCHES (96.5 X 45.7 CM)

Thrown and hand-built earthenware; electric fired, cone 04; clay slips, underglaze

PHOTO © ARTIST

Susie Bogard

Dream of Africa | 2004

10½ X 9 INCHES (26.7 X 22.9 CM)

Wheel-thrown and hand-built high-fire stoneware;
terra sigillata; saggar fired with steel wool,
copper carbonate salt, and wood shavings;
raku fired, 1600°F (871°C)

PHOTOS © ARTIST

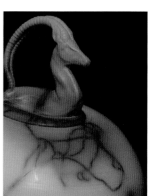

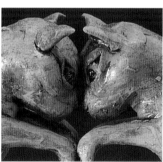

Susan Bostwick

Mysterious Moles | 2005

14 X 10 X 7 INCHES (35.6 X 25.4 X 17.8 CM)

Hand-built earthenware; electric fired,
cone 03; slips, stains, glazes

PHOTOS © JOSEPH GRUBER

Leland Shaw

Don't Feed the Bears | 2005

23 X 8 INCHES (58.4 X 20.3 CM)

Wheel-thrown terra cotta; fired in oxidation, cone 05; sprigged additions, glaze, terra sigillata

PHOTO © ARTIST

A very secretive little lizard hides in the upper handle. —*DCS*

Doris Clyde Slade

Hide and Seek | 2005

7 X 9 X 5½ INCHES (17.8 X 22.9 X 14 CM)

Wheel-thrown, hand-sculpted
and slab-built porcelain; celadon,
cone 10; stain, luster

PHOTOS © VINCE CASSARO

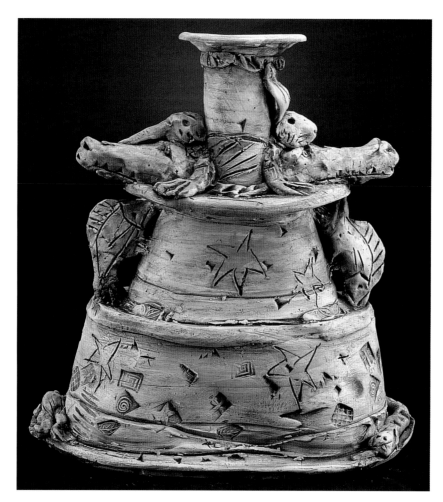

Dennis Sipiorski

Gators and Fish | 2000

36 X 20 X 8 INCHES (91.4 X 50.8 X 20.3 CM)

Thrown and hand-built red clay; electric
fired and salt fired, cone 6

PHOTO © ARTIST

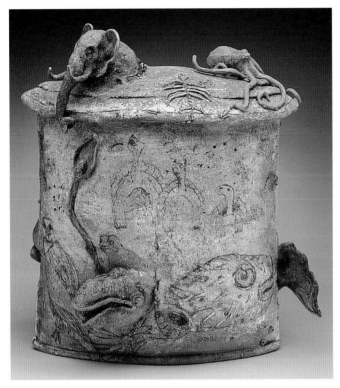

Delicate and superb, the juxtaposed drawn and sculpted images of Waking the Barnacle *transition into each other. Swan Morningstar Whigham simultaneously achieves a feeling of timelessness and the timely.* —JB

Swan Morningstar Whigham
Waking the Barnacle | 2005
13 X 11 X 9¾ INCHES (33 X 27.9 X 24.8 CM)
Hand-built stoneware; salt fired, cone 3
PHOTOS © WALKER MONTGOMERY

Tré Arenz

Bernadette of Lourdes | 2000

25 X 14 X 12½ INCHES (63.5 X 35.6 X 31.8 CM)

Hand-built clay; electric fired, cone 1; gold leaf

PHOTO © DAVID WHARTON
COURTESY OF WILLIAM CAMPBELL CONTEMPORARY ART, INC.

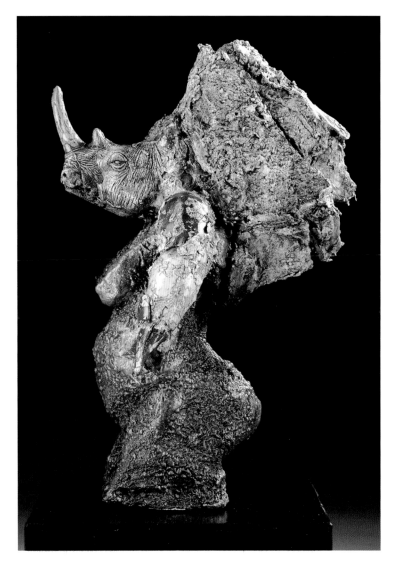

Christopher A. Vicini

Mother | 2003

10 X 20 X 8 INCHES (25.4 X 50.8 X 20.3 CM)

Hand-built and press-molded porcelain;
glaze; electric fired, cone 6

PHOTO © MARK JOHNSTON

Maria DeCastro

Avian Influence | 2005

19 X 5 X 4 INCHES (48.3 X 12.7 X 10.2 CM)

Hand-built and sculpted stoneware; single
fired; stamped; copper wash, wax

PHOTOS © ARTIST

Katy Rush

Bunny Masquerade Teapot | 2005

10 X 6 X 6 INCHES (25.4 X 15.2 X 15.2 CM)

Hand-built porcelain; electric fired, cone 6

PHOTO © DANIEL BARKER
COURTESY OF FERRIN GALLERY

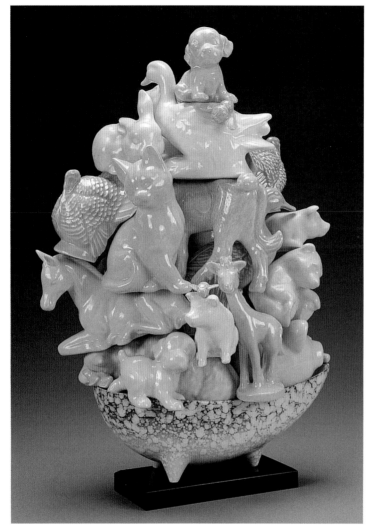

Ahimsa *is a Sanskrit
word meaning "non-
violence"; it stresses the
active avoidance of harm
and violence to sentient
beings, including ani-
mals. And though a
trophy is traditionally
an award for success in
competition and war, my*
Ahimsa Trophy *series
celebrates the preserva-
tion of life, compassion,
and kindness in the inter-
action between humans
and animals.* —WW

Wendy Walgate

Ahimsa Trophy Yellow | 2005

17 X 10 X 7 INCHES (43.2 X 25.4 X 17.8 CM)
Slip-cast white earthenware; cone 06;
vintage ceramic container

PHOTOS © ARTIST

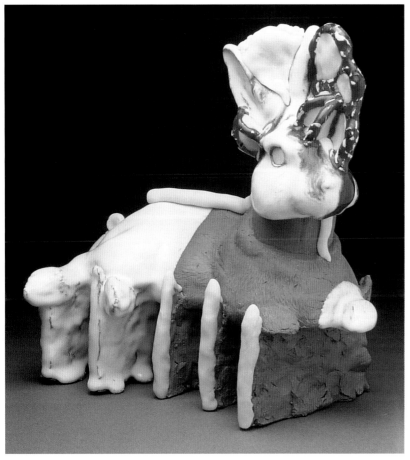

Elissa Armstrong

White Fantastic | 2004

10½ X 10½ X 7 INCHES (26.7 X 26.7 X 17.8 CM)
Hand-built earthenware; electric fired,
cone 04; glaze

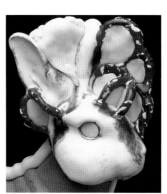

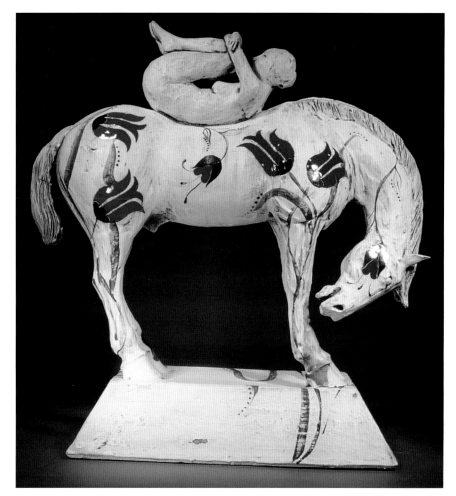

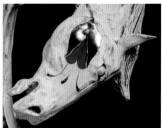

Sue Tirrell

Persian Rider | 2004

21 X 21 X 10 INCHES (53.3 X 53.3 X 25.4 CM)
Slab-built earthenware; electric fired,
cone 04; slip, terra sigillata, glazes,
underglazes, luster
PHOTOS © ARTIST

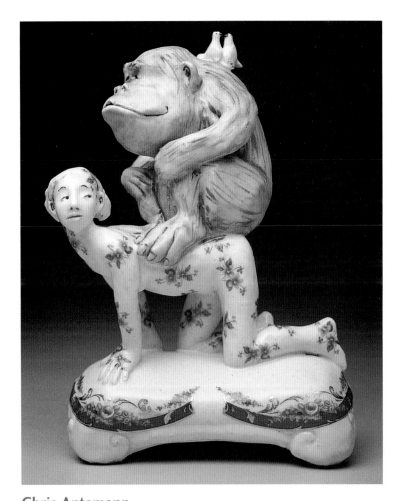

Chris Antemann

Monkey Rider | 2001

10 X 8 X 5 INCHES (25.4 X 20.3 X 12.7 CM)

Porcelain; cone 10; ceramic decals

PHOTO © ARTIST

Adelaide Paul is a master of expression and the detailed execution. Supraspinous is an anatomy lesson intending, I think, to elicit empathy with other species and to raise questions of morality as well. —JB

Adelaide Paul

Supraspinous | 2004

18 X 13 INCHES (45.7 X 33 CM)
Porcelain; leather

PHOTO COURTESY OF GARTH CLARK GALLERY, NY

Rytas Jakimavičius

Guarding Dog I | 2002

DOG, 10¼ X 4⅓ X 2 INCHES (26 X 11 X 5 CM);
HEAD, 2 X 4 2/3 X 2 INCHES (5 X 11 X 5 CM)

Hand-built porcelain; electric fired,
cone 6; gold, cone 016

PHOTO © ARTIST

Rebekah Bogard

Cloud Nine | 2005

29 X 41 X 30 INCHES (73.7 X 104.1 X 76.2 CM)

Slab-built and press-molded earthenware; electric fired, cone 04; underglaze, glaze, cone 04; oil paint, metal rods

Annette Corcoran's Banana Flower Teapot with Royal Flycatcher *is a wonderful example of simultaneity. The elements of the pot are very cleverly the elements of nature, and her color sensibility here conveys perfectly both the bird and its environment.* —JB

Annette Corcoran

Banana Flower Teapot with Royal Flycatcher | 2005

12½ X 11½ X 8 INCHES (31.8 X 29.2 X 20.3 CM)
Thrown and altered porcelain and stoneware; electric fired,
2000°F (1093°C), underglaze, glaze, overglaze

PHOTO © PATRICK TRAGENZA

Eunjung Park

Carp with Chameleon | 2004

12½ X 15 X 5½ INCHES (31.8 X 38.1 X 14 CM)

Slip-cast porcelain; electric fired, cone 8

PHOTO © ARTIST
COURTESY OF FERRIN GALLERY

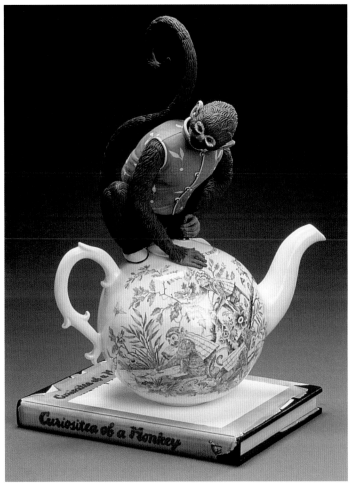

Red Weldon Sandlin's Curositea of a Monkey *is another in her punning series of teapots. The echo of the cobalt graphic ornamenting the belly of the teapot with the curious fellow above it is particularly well composed, and the shift in scale between the objects and the animal contributes to a "magic world" kind of view.* —JB

Red Weldon Sandlin
Curositea of a Monkey | 2001

10½ X 5½ X 11¼ INCHES (26.7 X 14 X 28.6 CM)
Slab and coil built; wood, acrylic paint; underglaze, engobe; bisque fired, cone 04; underglaze, glaze, cone 06

PHOTOS © CHARLEY AKERS
COURTESY OF FERRIN GALLERY

Asia Mathis

Rabbit in Sideways Split | 2003

22 X 22 X 10 INCHES (55.9 X 55.9 X 25.4 CM)

Slab-built porcelain; electric fired, cone 6

PHOTO © MICHAEL COTHRAN

Reed Weir

Boxer | 2003

20½ X 33¹/₁₆ X 11⁷/₁₆ INCHES (52 X 84 X 29 CM)

Hand-built, coil-built, and soft-slab stoneware;
electric fired, cone 6; metal spring

PHOTO © DAVID MORRISH

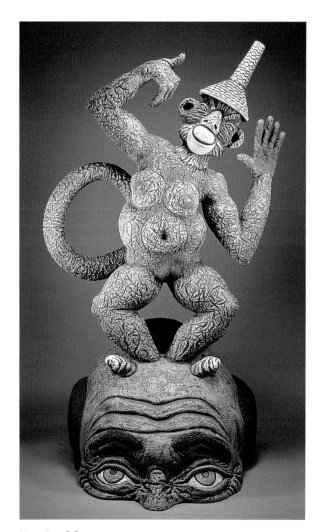

Jim Budde

Red | 2002

30 X 16 X 12 INCHES (76.2 X 40.6 X 30.5 CM)

Slab-built stoneware; electric fired,
cone 3; glaze, cone 08

PHOTO © ARTIST
COLLECTION OF DIANE AND SANDY BESSER

Surrealistic and postmodernist, Lisa Clague's masterful work exploits the inherent possibilities of glaze surface to enhance form and amplify meaning. Clague's lyrical imagination is powerfully evident here. —JB

Lisa Clague
In the Nature of Things | 2004

75 X 48 X 16 INCHES (190.5 X 121.9 X 40.6 CM)
Coil built; metal, glazes, stains, wax, cone 04

PHOTO © TOM MILLS

Melody Ellis

Choose a Hand | 2003

7 X 5 X 8 INCHES (17.8 X 12.7 X 20.3 CM)

Hand-built earthenware; electric fired,
cone 04; steel pins

PHOTO © ARTIST

Janis Mars Wunderlich's work is always dense and rich with texture, color, and pattern as well as a kind of dark and surreal personal vision. Here, her signature playfulness contains only a hint of the macabre. —JB

Janis Mars Wunderlich
Family Pet | 2005

17 X 9 X 20 INCHES (43.2 X 22.9 X 50.8 CM)
Hand-built earthenware; cone 3; slip, underglaze, overglaze, cone 04
PHOTOS © ARTIST

*Like an African
Atlas, Denise
Romecki's rhino bears
a threatened world,
revealed in meticulous
clay craft.* —JB

Denise Romecki

Last Sanctuary | 2000

19 X 12 X 27 INCHES (48.3 X 30.5 X 68.6 CM)
Slab-built and sculpted stoneware; electric fired,
cone 2; underglaze, glaze, oxides, cone 05

PHOTOS © JERRY ANTHONY

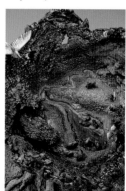

Dina Wilde-Ramsing

Bull with Pets | 2005

16 X 17 X 7 INCHES (40.6 X 43.2 X 17.8 CM)

Slab- and coil-built red earthenware;
oxidation fired, cone 03; underglaze,
oxide washes, terra sigillata

PHOTO © SCOTT TAYLOR

Etta Winigrad

The Gathering | 2000

8 X 17 X 17 INCHES (20.3 X 43.2 X 43.2 CM)

Hand-built low-fire white talc;
electric fired, cone 02; smoked

PHOTO © ARTIST

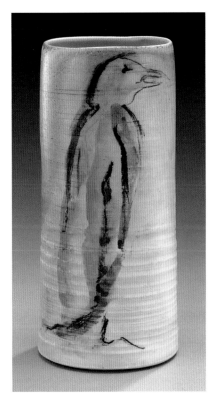

Peggy Forman
Jan Schachter

Bird | 2004

8¼ X 3½ X 3½ INCHES (21 X 8.9 X 8.9 CM)
Thrown porcelain; gas fired, cone 10,
cone 05; underglaze pencils,
stains, slips

PHOTO © HAP SAKWA

Ira Winarsky

Gooseware | 1989

1 X 11¼ INCHES (2.5 X 28.6 CM)
Wheel-thrown stoneware; electric fired, cone 10

PHOTO © ARTIST

Though greatly diminished, fierce Cerberus appears here to still have a duty to protect a hidden world. Could the residue of Greek Hades lurk within this refined porcelain pot by Susan Greenleaf? —JB

Susan Greenleaf
Cerberus | 1996

12 X 12 INCHES (30.5 X 30.5 CM)
Wheel-thrown and modeled porcelain;
celadon glaze, cone 10

PHOTO © RICHARD RODRIQUEZ

This piece pays homage to the fur used to create brush tips. A custom-created rabbit hairbrush was used to paint the black underglaze mark of the rabbit image. —GG

Glenn Grishkoff

Rabbit Brush Bouquet | 2005

18 X 30 X 9 INCHES (45.7 X 76.2 X 22.9 CM)

Wheel-thrown and coil-built porcelain; raku fired, cone 06; brush handles, coarse garnet dust, horse mane hair

PHOTOS © MARK LAMOREAUX
COURTESY OF THE ART SPIRIT GALLERY OF FINE ART, COEUR D'ALENE, ID

Michael Simon

Square Dish, Added Rim with White Fish | 2003

3 X 12 X 12 INCHES (7.6 X 30.5 X 30.5 CM)

Wheel-thrown and altered earthenware; salt fired

PHOTO © ARTIST
COURTESY OF THE SIGNATURE SHOP & GALLERY, ATLANTA, GA

Ann Gleason

Rooster Platter | 2005

14 X 2 INCHES (35.6 X 5.1 CM)

Wheel-thrown stoneware; electric fired,
cone 6; slip, clear glaze

PHOTO © TIM BARNWELL

Laura O'Donnell

Fish Plate | 2004

2 X 10 X 8 INCHES (5.1 X 25.4 X 20.3 CM)

Press-molded dark stoneware; gas
fired in reduction, cone 10

PHOTO © CHRIS BERTI

Ilena Finocchi

Fearlessness of Youth | 2005

8 X 18 X 18 INCHES (20.3 X 45.7 X 45.7 CM)
Hand-built and press-molded earthenware;
smoke fired, cone 04; terra sigillata,
lost-wax cast bronze

PHOTO © ED BERNIK

Pam Owens

Sheep Jar | 2000

8 X 4 X 4 INCHES (20.3 X 10.2 X 10.2 CM)
Wheel-thrown and hand-sculpted
stoneware; wood fired, cone 10
PHOTO © TIM AYERS

Delyth Jones

Ram–Sheep | 2004

3⁹⁄₁₆ X 1⁹⁄₁₆ X 4¾ INCHES (9 X 4 X 12 CM)
Slab-built white earthenware; bisque fired,
1976°F (1080°C); smoke fired
PHOTO © ARTIST

Myth and mystery are evoked by Shari McWilliams's exacting attention to detail. Her combination of alligator and horse evoke prehistoric associations. —JB

Shari McWilliams

Swamp Fever | 2005

13 X 9 X 18 INCHES (33 X 22.9 X 45.7 CM)
Slab-built stoneware; gas fired in
reduction, cone 6; engobes

PHOTO © ARTIST

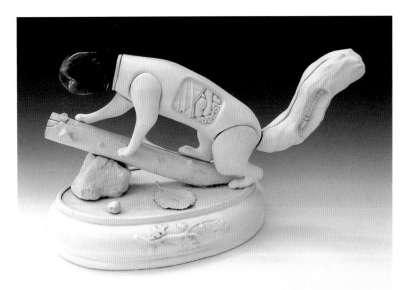

John Byrd

Squirrel | 2003

22 X 17 INCHES (55.9 X 43.2 CM)
Ceramic; taxidermic materials
PHOTO COURTESY OF GARTH CLARK GALLERY, NY

Beth Cavener Stichter

One Last Word | 2005

24 X 15 INCHES (61 X 38.1 CM)
Stoneware; porcelain slip, steel
PHOTO COURTESY OF GARTH CLARK GALLERY, NY

Debra Bacianga

Monkey Mind | 2005

13 X 6½ X 14 INCHES (33 X 16.5 X 35.6 CM)

Hand-built stoneware; electric fired,
cone 5; glaze, cone 05½

PHOTOS © LISA ALHBERG

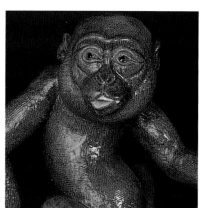

Etta Winigrad

The Guardian | 1997

30 X 14 X 5 INCHES (76.2 X 35.6 X 12.7 CM)

Hand-built low-fire white talc;
electric fired, cone 02; smoked

PHOTO © ARTIST

Much of my recent work has focused on the relationship between dogs and people. This piece shows the dog as product: custom designed and mass-produced, and subject to the whims of fads and fashion. —CA

Cheryl Andrews

Evolution | 2005

24 X 16 INCHES (61 X 40.6 CM)
Slab- and coil-built white earthenware;
electric fired, cone 2; stains, acrylic paint

PHOTOS © STEVE MANN

Denise Romecki

A Delicate Balance | 2001

57 X 16 X 23 INCHES (144.8 X 40.6 X 58.4 CM)

Slab-built and sculpted stoneware; electric fired, cone 2; underglaze, glaze, cone 05; acrylic paint, metal rods

PHOTO © JERRY ANTHONY

Dalia Laučkaitė-Jakimavičienė

Mouse Box | 2005

13 X 11¹³⁄₁₆ X 6⁵⁄₁₆ INCHES (33 X 30 X 16 CM)
Slab-built earthenware; electric fired, cone 01;
custom computer-rendered laser decals,
cone 08; commercial decals, china paint,
gold, luster, cone 015

PHOTO © VIDMANTAS ILCIUKAS

Folk art-inspired, with echoes of Mexican (especially Nayarit) and Han dynasty house pottery, this bird-protected structure by Anne Bernard-Pattis has charm to spare. —JB

Anne Bernard-Pattis

Sheltered by Birds | 2005

13 X 6 X 5 INCHES (33 X 15.2 X 12.7 CM)
Thrown and altered dark stoneware;
electric fired, cone 10

PHOTOS © WILLIAM BIDERBOST

David Regan

TH2000 | 2004

17½ X 27 INCHES (44.5 X 68.6 CM)

Porcelain

PHOTOS COURTESY OF GARTH CLARK GALLERY, NY

The realities of life as food chain. John Byrd presents an excellent example of glaze's power to elicit simultaneous realities—the frozen liquidity of the glaze and the sticky wetness of bodily fluids. —JB

John Byrd

Coyote with Squirrel | 2002

33 X 47 X 16 INCHES (83.8 X 119.4 X 40.6 CM)
Mixed media

Carrianne Hendrickson

Commission Based on Darwin's Origin of Species (Untitled) | 2004

24 X 17 X 14 INCHES (61 X 43.2 X 35.6 CM)

Hand-built and hollowed low-fire white clay; cone 04; low-fire glaze, underglaze

PHOTOS © ARTIST

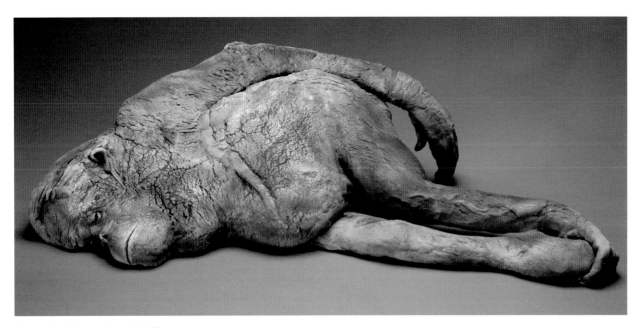

Pamela Earnshaw Kelly

Resting | 2004

8 X 34 X 21 INCHES (20.3 X 86.4 X 53.3 CM)
Slab-built raku clay; raku fired, cone 05

PHOTO © ARTIST

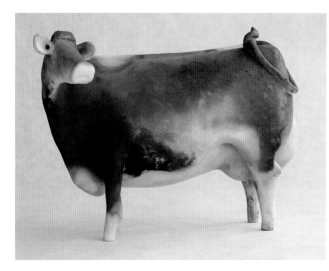

Delyth Jones's Cow, which suggests a Holstein, is charming in its simple, naïve modeling. The usually random and unpredictable patterning of a smoked surface is here effectively controlled along the body contours. —JB

Delyth Jones

Cow | 2004

6⁵⁄₁₆ X 2³⁄₈ X 8¹⁄₄ INCHES (16 X 6 X 21 CM)
Slab-built white earthenware; bisque fired,
1976°F (1080°C); smoke fired
PHOTO © ARTIST

Phyllis A. Kaye

Terry | 2004

14¹⁄₂ X 8¹⁄₂ X 12¹⁄₂ INCHES (36.8 X 21.6 X 31.8 CM)
Hand-built clay; electric fired, cone 06;
glaze, cone 6; acrylic
PHOTO © BILIANA POPOVA

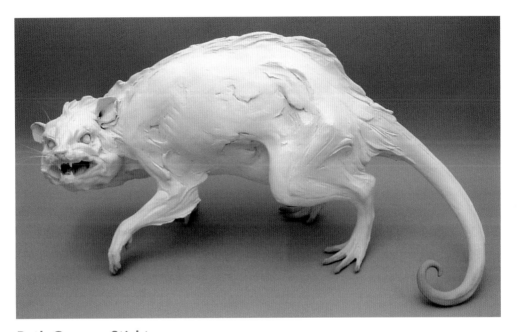

Beth Cavener Stichter

Please | 2005

14 X 27 INCHES (35.6 X 68.6 CM)
Stoneware; porcelain slip
PHOTO COURTESY OF GARTH CLARK GALLERY, NY

The "break" that embellishes the shino glaze on Emily Dyer's little lizard is perfect. —JB

Emily Dyer

Lizard Bowl | 2004

7 X 4 INCHES (17.8 X 10.2 CM)

Wheel-thrown and press-molded Laguna B-mix;
gas fired in reduction, cone 10

PHOTO © PETRONELLA J. YTSMA

Susan Bostwick

Defying Solomon | 2005

16 X 10 X 7 INCHES (40.6 X 25.4 X 17.8 CM)

Hand-built earthenware; electric fired,
cone 03; slips, stains, glazes

PHOTO © JOSEPH GRUBER

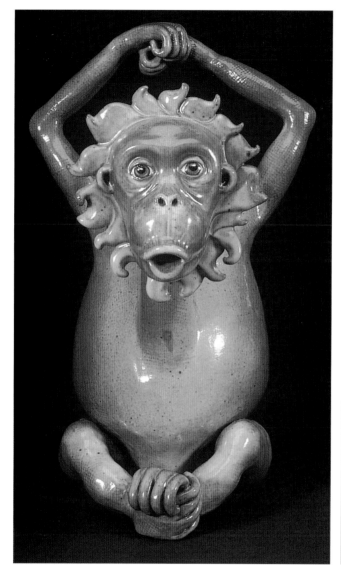

Annette Kirma

Monkey Watering Pitcher | 2004

16 X 10 X 18 INCHES (40.6 X 25.4 X 45.7 CM)
Thrown, coil- and slab-built stoneware;
gas fired, cone 10; shino glaze

PHOTOS © RICHEY BELLINGER

Lisa Clague
Mark Peters

Striped Monkey | 2005

17 X 8 X 8 INCHES (43.2 X 20.3 X 20.3 CM)
Mixed media
PHOTO © ARTISTS

Outstanding craft and skill are here at the service of a transposed plot; is this the truth about little Red Riding Hood, or is it wishful thinking? This discreet piece is only one element in Cynthia Consentino's consummate execution in the art of installation. —JB

Cynthia Consentino

Wolf Girl I | 2001

42 X 16 X 16 INCHES (106.7 X 40.6 X 40.6 CM)
Clay, oils, cold wax
PHOTO © ARTIST

Red Weldon Sandlin

To Tease a Mockingbird Teapots | 2002

14 X 22 X 7 INCHES (35.6 X 55.9 X 17.8 CM)
Slab-built white earthenware; cone 04;
hand painted underglaze, oxide, cone 06

PHOTOS © CHARLEY AKERS
COURTESY OF FERRIN GALLERY

Jim Koudelka

John Deer Jar | 2001

21 X 18 X 13 INCHES (53.3 X 45.7 X 33 CM)

Assembled, thrown, and press-molded
stoneware clay; multi-fired, cone 10,
cone 04, cone 06

PHOTO © ARTIST

Comic and a little goofy, Annette Kirma's Rhino Watering Can *would amuse with every use. Her contrast of elegant formal elements (a twisted bail handle) and cartoonish representation (of legs and toes) is unified by the zoomorphic form.* —JB

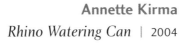

Annette Kirma
Rhino Watering Can | 2004

15 X 7 X 18 INCHES (38.1 X 17.8 X 45.7 CM)
Thrown, coil-, and slab-built stoneware;
gas fired, cone 10; glaze

PHOTOS © RICHEY BELLINGER

Constance Sherman

Dragon Tureen | 2005

12 X 15 X 6 INCHES (30.5 X 38.1 X 15.2 CM)
Wheel-thrown and assembled; gas fired
in reduction, cone 10

PHOTO © HOWARD GOODMAN

Amy Shook

Protector | 2004

6 X 16 X 12 INCHES (15.2 X 40.6 X 30.5 CM)
Thrown and hand-built stoneware;
anagama fired, cone 10

PHOTO © TIM BARNWELL

Jennifer Orchard

Urban Mis-take (AKA Rosy) | 2004

17¾ X 9⅞ X 19¹¹⁄₁₆ INCHES (45 X 25 X 50 CM)

Slip-cast earthenware; electric fired, cone 01,
cone 04; glaze, underglaze

PHOTO © ARTIST

Scott Causey

Dog | 2005

26 X 14 X 28 INCHES (66 X 35.6 X 71.1 CM)

Slip-cast white earthenware; electric
fired, cone 05 1/2; multifired,
cone 06; lusters, cone 018; epoxy

PHOTO © ARTIST

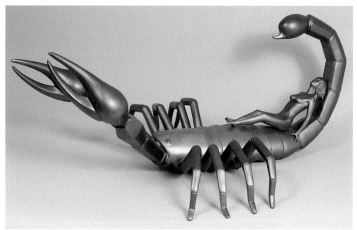

Jack Thompson, AKA Jugo de Vegetales

Scorpio | 2005

20 X 30 X 48 INCHES (50.8 X 76.2 X 121.9 CM)

Cast and modeled paper clay; electric fired, cone 05;
bronze powders, graphite, alkyd medium

PHOTO © ARTIST

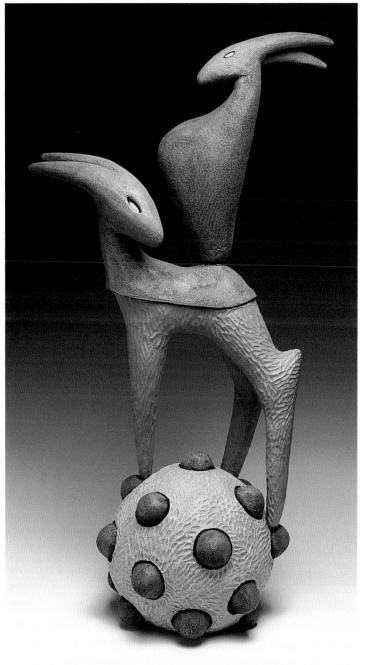

Abstracted and stylized, these Goats on Parade, by Bryan Hiveley, might be auditioning for Cirque du Soleil. They are handsome in their smooth coats, and nicely set off by the textured carving: they look ready to perform. —JB

Bryan Hiveley

Goats on Parade | 2005

30 X 17 X 10 INCHES (76.2 X 43.2 X 25.4 CM)
Coil-built earthenware; electric fired, cone 03

PHOTO © ARTIST

Suzy Birstein

Spirit Bottle: Two aMuse | 2002

13 X 10 X 7 INCHES (33 X 25.4 X 17.8 CM)

Hand-built whiteware; electric fired, cone 01;
underglazes, glazes, acrylic paint, cone 05

PHOTOS © KEN MAYER

> *David Cooke's touch is natural and languid; the clay is draped in a perfect imitation of the natural grace of the lizard's body.* —JB

David Cooke

Monitor Lizard | 2004

25⁹⁄₁₆ X 39³⁄₈ X 18½ INCHES (65 X 100 X 47 CM)

Coil built, slab built; crank,
2282°F (1250°C); metal oxides

PHOTO © ARTIST

Elaine Bolz

Raven Column | 2003

19 X 9 X 6 INCHES (48.3 X 22.9 X 15.2 CM)

Slab-built and sculpted white
earthenware; electric fired, cone 02;
airbrushed underglaze, glaze, cone 05

PHOTO © MARGO GEIST

Humorous and elegant at the same time, this unglazed earthenware teapot by Hwang Jeng-daw, with its traces of art nouveau design, also has a hint of Assyrian relief. —JB

Hwang Jeng-daw
Cock Teapot | 2004

6 11/16 X 6 11/16 X 1 9/16 INCHES (17 X 14 X 7 CM)
Cast earthenware; electric fired, cone 8
PHOTO © ARTIST

Silvie Granatelli
Swan Oil Ewer | 2003

7 X 4 1/2 X 4 1/2 INCHES (17.8 X 11.4 X 11.4 CM)
Wheel-thrown and altered porcelain;
gas fired, cone 10
PHOTO © TIM BARNWELL

James Tingey

Sandhill Crane | 2005

11 X 6 X 6 INCHES (27.9 X 15.2 X 15.2 CM)

Wheel-thrown porcelain; gas fired,
cone 10; sgraffito

PHOTO © ARTIST

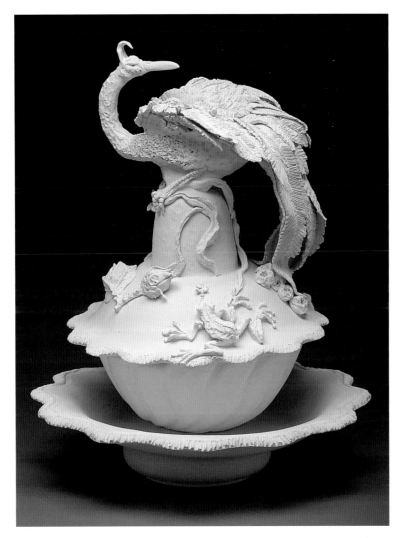

A precise geometry of pottery form supports the expressive modeling of Genya Glass's animal narrative. She's made astute use of the pot as support and foil to her textured modeling. —JB

Genya Glass

Bird of Paradise | 2005

18 X 17 INCHES (45.8 X 43.2 CM)
Altered slump-molded vessel; hand-built creatures

PHOTO © ERIC NORBOM

Susan Bell

Owl | 2005

14 X 8 X 8 INCHES (35.6 X 20.3 X 20.3 CM)
Hand-built raku clay; electric fired, cone 06;
hand-painted underglazes, glazes, cone 06
PHOTO © ARTIST

This piece is meant to illustrate a mental picture I had of a shaggy dog infested with people doing things—watching TV, having a picnic, throwing a party, climbing, swimming, and so on—all going about their business with no awareness of the larger body. —CA

Cheryl Andrews
Another Shaggy Dog Story | 2004

16½ X 16½ X 11½ INCHES (41.9 X 41.9 X 29.2 CM)
Coil- and slab-built stoneware; gas fired,
cone 10; shino, luster

PHOTOS © STEVE MANN

Robin Sadek Ascher

Goose Container | 2005

12 X 6½ X 17 INCHES (30.5 X 16.5 X 43.2 CM)
Slab-built terra cotta; bisque fired,
cone 06; underglaze
PHOTO © JOSEPH GIUNTA

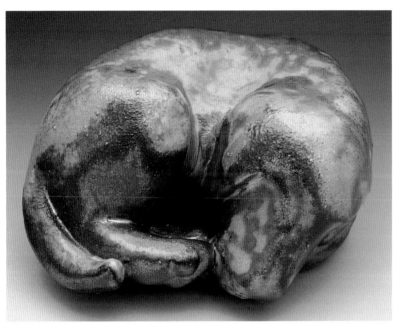

Glaze color and surface embellish and camouflage this otherwise muted form by K. Sam Miller, yet the familiar and the exotic are effectively combined. —JB

K. Sam Miller

Dog Dreams | 2005

2½ X 2½ X 2½ INCHES (6.4 X 6.4 X 6.4 CM)
Hand-pinched stoneware; gas fired in reduction, cone 10; multiple sprayed glazes

PHOTOS © HARRISON EVANS

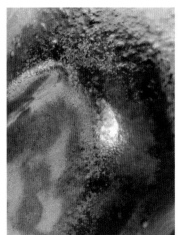

Lesley Martin

Jade Horse Head | 2003

13¾ X 11¹³⁄₁₆ X 5⅞ INCHES (35 X 30 X 15 CM)

Slab-built stoneware, paper clay; raku fired

PHOTO © ARTIST

Lindsey de Ovies

Untitled | 2004

3 X 2¾ INCHES (7.6 X 7 CM)

Hand-built clay; gouache, wax patina

PHOTO © WALKER MONTGOMERY

Mary J. Sweeney

Untitled | 2004

18 X 6 X 6 INCHES (45.7 X 15.2 X 15.2 CM)

Hand-built earthenware; saggar fired bisque,
cone 06; terra sigillata

PHOTO © ARTIST

Novie Trump

Bird Tower | 2005

14 X 13½ X 2 INCHES (35.6 X 34.3 X 5.1 CM)
Hand-built clay; gas fired, cone 10; glazes
PHOTO © GREG STALEY

Louis Mendez

Minoan Bull | 1965

8¾ X 12 X 4½ INCHES (22.2 X 30.5 X 11.4 CM)

Hand-built stoneware clay; gas fired in
reduction, cone 10; oxides

PHOTO © JAMES DEE

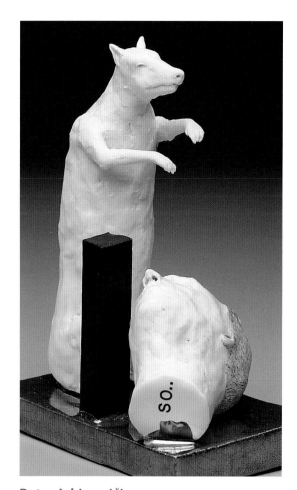

Rytas Jakimavičius

Guarding Dog II | 2002

7⅞ X 3½ X 5¹⁵⁄₁₆ INCHES (20 X 9 X 15 CM)

Hand-built porcelain; electric fired,
cone 6; decals, gold, cone 016

PHOTO © ARTIST

Sue Tirrell

Honyoker's Horse | 2004

18 X 16 X 8 INCHES (45.7 X 40.6 X 20.3 CM)

Slab-built earthenware; electric fired,
cone 04; terra sigillata, underglazes, glaze

PHOTO © ARTIST

*My first ocarina, given to me by a friend, was small, high-pitched, and beautifully
tuned. I learned to play by imitating birds and listening to their response echo
around the clearing where we lived. Over time, I began making ocarinas, which—like
the whale—are larger, deeper toned, and have a more meditative resonance.* —RR

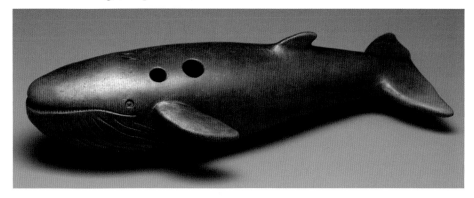

Ron Robb

Whale Ocarina | 2005

2½ X 4 X 10 INCHES (6.4 X 10.2 X 25.4 CM)
Hand-formed and press-molded; gas
fired, cone 06; burnished, terra
sigillata; post-fire reduction
PHOTO © DAVID MOLYNEAUX

Diana Pittis

Trout | 2005

9¼ X 21¾ X 4¾ INCHES (23.5 X 55.2 X 12.1 CM)
Slab-built stoneware; raku fired, cone 05; concrete
PHOTO © MIKE KELLER

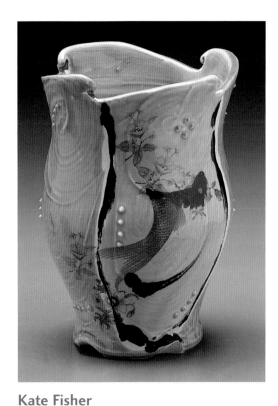

Kate Fisher

The Coy Vase | 2005

10 X 4 X 4 INCHES (25.4 X 10.2 X 10.2 CM)

Wheel-thrown porcelain; oxidation fired, cone 6; decals, cone 017

PHOTO © STEVE SCHNIEDER

Laura McKibbon

Ostrich Casserole | 2005

10 X 7 X 1½ INCHES (25.4 X 17.8 X 3.8 CM)

Slab-built terra cotta; electric fired, cone 04; silkscreened underglaze transfer

PHOTO © ARTIST

Bryan Hiveley

Rabbit Platter | 2002

18 X 18 X 7 INCHES (45.7 X 45.7 X 17.8 CM)

Hand-built earthenware; electric fired, cone 03

PHOTO © ARTIST

Cris Conklin

Margarita Glass | 2005

5½ X 4½ X 4½ INCHES (14 X 11.4 X 11.4 CM)

Thrown white stoneware; gas fired,
cone 10; slip, sgraffito

PHOTO © GLENN ASAKAWA

Tim Christensen-Kirby

Changes Coming | 2005

6 X 4 X 4 INCHES (15.2 X 10.2 X 10.2 CM)

Wheel-thrown porcelain; propane fired,
cone 7; oxides, sgraffito

PHOTO © ARTIST

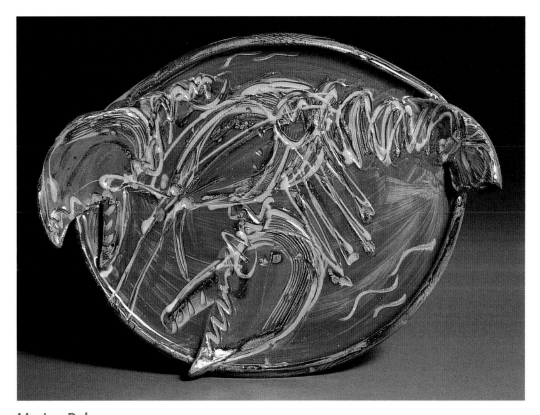

Marian Baker

Lobster Platter | 2004

2 X 13 X 11 INCHES (5.1 X 33 X 27.9 CM)

Thrown and altered stoneware; gas fired,
cone 10; slips, soda fired

PHOTO © ARTIST

Annette Corcoran

Jade Teapot with Brown Hooded Parrot | 2005

17 X 11½ X 8 INCHES (43.2 X 29.2 X 20.3 CM)

Thrown and altered porcelain and stoneware;
electric fired, 2000°F (1093°C); underglaze,
glaze, overglaze

Mythic residue and a hint of bestiality are subordinate to the affection and inter-species love apparent in this rendering by Jenny Mendes. Folk art borrowings and deliberate guilelessness are convincingly manipulated with sweet effect. —JB

Jenny Mendes

Horseman | 2005

8 X 7 X 4 INCHES (20.3 X 17.8 X 10.2 CM)
Coil-built terra cotta; electric fired,
cone 03; terra sigillata

PHOTO © JERRY ANTHONY

Karl Kuhns

Debra Parker-Kuhns

White Dog Pot | 2004

8 X 6 X 6 INCHES (20.3 X 15.2 X 15.2 CM)

Wheel-thrown and hand-built porcelain; electric fired,
cone 8; polychrome slips, clear glaze

PHOTO © ARTISTS

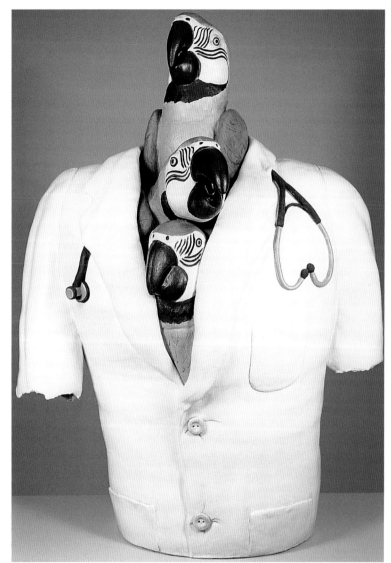

Cynthia Siegel

Modern Medicine | 2003

35 X 24 X 15 INCHES (88.9 X 61 X 38.1 CM)

Coil-built white stoneware; gas fired, cone 05;
commercial glazes and underglazes, cone 02

PHOTOS © STAN EINHORN AND ARTIST

Helen Tiley

Tiger and Girl | 2005

7 7/8 X 14 3/16 X 11 INCHES (20 X 36 X 28 CM)

Hand-built white earthenware; electric fired, 2048°F (1120°C); slip, 1940°F (1060°C); luster, 1382°F (750°C)

PHOTO © JO PASCOE

Carrianne Hendrickson presents a sweetly lyrical version of the story of McGee, an 18th-century Scottish-American who embraced two Native American tribes. She employs iconographic images to mythologize his life and marriage to a Choctaw woman. —JB

Carrianne Hendrickson
Malcolm McGee and the Three White Beasts | 2001

27 X 12 X 15 INCHES (68.6 X 30.5 X 38.1 CM)
Hand-built and hollowed low-fire clay; electric fired,
cone 04; gouache, wax, low-fire glaze

PHOTOS © ARTIST

Janis Mars Wunderlich
Puppy Child | 2003

16 X 10 X 11 INCHES (40.6 X 25.4 X 27.9 CM)

Hand-built earthenware; cone 3; slip,
underglaze, overglaze, cone 04

PHOTOS © ARTIST

Jane Peiser

Woman Riding Elephant Dime Bank | 1996

8 X 7 X 7 INCHES (20.3 X 17.8 X 17.8 CM)
Hand-built porcelain; cone 10; salt overglaze
PHOTO © TOM MILLS

Laura DeAngelis

Acrobat | 2002

34 X 24 X 11 INCHES (86.4 X 61 X 27.9 CM)

Engobes, wood ash glaze, multifired, cone 04

PHOTO © MATTHEW MCFARLAND

I wanted to capture the love some people have for their pets, an obsessive love that sometimes is taken to excessive and unnatural ends. —FN

Frances Norton

Dog Smooch | 1998

5 5/16 X 5 5/16 X 5 5/16 INCHES (15 X 15 X 15 CM)

Hand-built and cast stoneware, slip, and paper clay; gas fired in reduction; wire armature, oxides, clear glaze

PHOTOS © ARTIST

Laura O'Donnell

Grasshopper Plate | 2005

2 X 12 INCHES (5.1 X 30.5 CM)

Wheel-thrown earthenware; electric fired,
cone 02; sgraffito slip

PHOTO © CHRIS BERTI

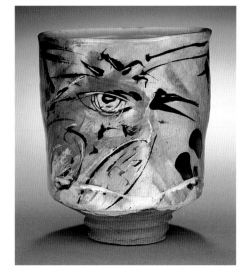

Ron Meyers

Unomi | 2005

4½ X 3 INCHES (11.4 X 7.6 CM)

Wheel-thrown earthenware; gas fired,
cone 04; underglazes, transparent glaze

PHOTO © W. MONTGOMERY

Added Rim Bowl with White Bird, *by Michael Simon, exemplifies this potter's deft mastery of the integration of two- and three-dimensional elements.* —JB

Michael Simon

Added Rim Bowl with White Bird | 2003

4½ X 16 X 13 INCHES (11.4 X 40.6 X 33 CM)

Wheel-thrown and altered earthenware; salt fired

Ron Myers's signature style in this leering rabbit updates a legacy of the best of the 20th-century expressionists. His casual painting approach is tempered by a mastery of means, for a virtuoso performance. —JB

Ron Meyers

Bowl | 2005

5 X 15 INCHES (12.7 X 38.1 CM)
Wheel-thrown earthenware; gas fired, cone 04;
underglazes, transparent glaze

PHOTO © W. MONTGOMERY

Jenny Lind

Pecos Field with Horses | 2005

20 X 4 INCHES (50.8 X 10.2 CM)

Molded stoneware; electric fired, cone 6;
underglaze, clear glaze

PHOTO © WENDY MCEAHERN
COURTESY OF RAINBOW GATE, SANTA FE, NEW MEXICO

Swan Morningstar Whigham

The Ark | 2005

9 1/4 X 19 X 6 1/2 INCHES (23.5 X 48.3 X 16.5 CM)

Hand-built stoneware; salt fired, cone 3

PHOTOS © WALKER MONTGOMERY

Ann Gleason

Hen | 2003

11 X 14 X 8½ INCHES (27.9 X 35.6 X 21.6 CM)

Coil-built stoneware; electric fired,
cone 6; slips, sgraffito, clear glaze

PHOTO © TIM BARNWELL

Zoomorphic form and reductive design reveal a simple and elegant bird pot by Anne-Beth Borselius. It's a good example of a pot form that suggests food service. —JB

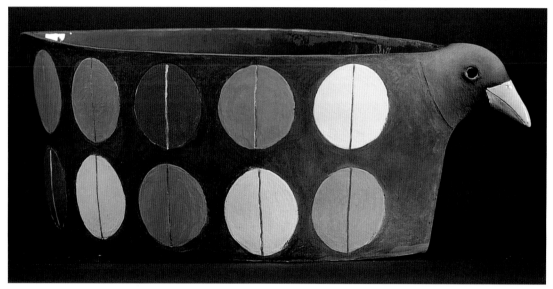

Anne-Beth Borselius
Dark Bird-Vessel | 2004

5½ X 13⅜ X 5⁵⁄₁₆ INCHES (14 X 34 X 13.5 CM)
Hand-built earthenware, electric fired,
cone 04; slips, burnished, partly glazed
PHOTOS © PEO ERIKSSON

Bruce Grimes

Raku Trout-Covered Jar | 2005

11 X 9 INCHES (27.9 X 22.9 CM)

Wheel-thrown stoneware; electric fired,
cone 06; raku fired

PHOTO © MEL MITTER MILLER

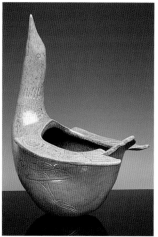

Michael Fromme

Ghost Loon 1 and 2 | 1996

LARGEST, 15 X 9½ X 11½ INCHES (38.1 X 24.1 X 29.2 CM)
Carved, slab built, coil built; anagama wood fired

PHOTOS © DENNIS MAXWELL

Nancy Halter
Greg Jahn

Beaked Pitcher with Fantasy Bird | 2005

PITCHER, 9¾ X 7 X 4½ INCHES (24.8 X 17.8 X 11.4 CM);
TEA BOWLS, EACH 4 X 3½ X 3½ INCHES (10.2 X 8.9 X 8.9 CM)

Thrown and altered porcelain; gas fired,
cone 10; underglaze

PHOTO © GREG JAHN

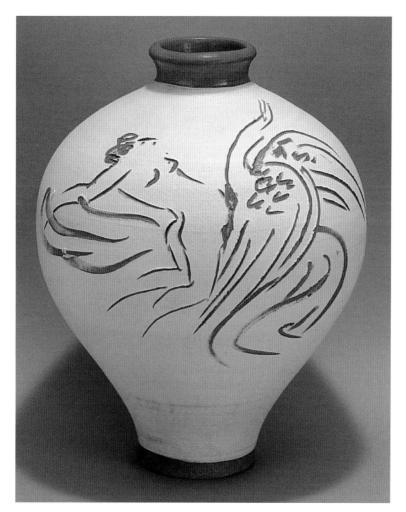

Reuben Nakian

Leda and the Swan Vase | 1982

14 X 19 INCHES (35.6 X 48.3 CM)

Earthenware

PHOTO COURTESY OF GARTH CLARK GALLERY, NY

Ira Winarsky

Gooseware | 1993

2 X 9½ INCHES (5.1 X 24.1 CM)

Wheel-thrown stoneware; electric
fired, cone 10

PHOTO © ARTIST

Michelle Erickson

The Peaceable Kingdom | 2005

17½ X 18 INCHES (44.5 X 45.7 CM)

Porcelain

PHOTO COURTESY OF GARTH CLARK GALLERY, NY

Diana Pittis

Striped Bass | 2004

11¼ X 16¾ X 6½ INCHES (28.6 X 42.5 X 16.5 CM)

Slab-built stoneware; raku fired,
cone 05; concrete

PHOTO © MIKE KELLER

*"Geobirds" are active
little insect-eaters from
the same family as the New
Zealand kiwi. They make their
nests from gold nuggets they
find in streams.* —GT

Geoffrey Tjakra

Geobird | 2005

7 X 4½ X 3 INCHES (17.8 X 11.4 X 7.6 CM)

Extruded, altered, and hand-built stoneware
and porcelain; gas, cone 5 and 10,
reduction; oxide wash, wire, plumbing tape,
panty-hose, thread

PHOTO © ARTIST

Tim Christensen-Kirby

Ivory Bill | 2005

12 X 12 X 1 INCHES (30.5 X 30.5 X 2.5 CM)

Wheel-thrown porcelain; propane fired,
cone 7; oxides, sgraffito

PHOTO © ARTIST

Laura Jean McLaughlin

Columbus Landing | 1995

18 X 14 X 4 INCHES (45.7 X 35.6 X 10.2 CM)

Slab-built white stoneware; slips, glazes, sgraffito

PHOTO © LONNIE GRAHAM

Kari K. Rives

Cone Dog | 2005

3 X 1¼ X 4¼ INCHES (7.6 X 3.2 X 10.8 CM)

Stoneware; electric fired, cone 5

PHOTO © ARTIST

Beth Cavener Stichter

Megrim | 2005

30 X 45 X 18 INCHES (76.2 X 114.3 X 45.7 CM)

Stoneware; cone 2; antique yoke, rope, forged iron rings, pulleys, rusted steel

PHOTOS © ARTIST

K. Sam Miller

Elephant Dreams | 2005

3 X 3 X 4 INCHES (7.6 X 7.6 X 10.2 CM)

Hand-pinched stoneware; gas fired in
reduction, cone 10; multiple sprayed glazes

PHOTO © HARRISON EVANS

Sara Molyneaux

Untitled | 2004

9 X 18 X 7 INCHES (22.9 X 45.7 X 17.8 CM)

Thrown, altered and hand-built stoneware;
electric fired, cone 06; glazes, luster

PHOTO © TOM HOLT

Bill Evans

Black Rhino | 2004

7 X 5 X 13 INCHES (17.8 X 12.7 X 33 CM)

Hand-built stoneware; gas fired,
cone 6; slip, soda fired

PHOTO © ARTIST

Architecture and archeology seem wedded to each other in this work. The figure of the horse, with its allusions to Troy and to all horse art, stands solidly, as if excavated from the earth itself. Jean-Pierre Larocque conjures from his clay the simultaneous impression of modernity and antiquity. —JB

Jean-Pierre Larocque
Untitled Horse with House | 2004

32 X 30 X 14 INCHES (81.3 X 76.2 X 35.6 CM)
Stoneware
PHOTO COURTESY OF GARTH CLARK GALLERY, NY

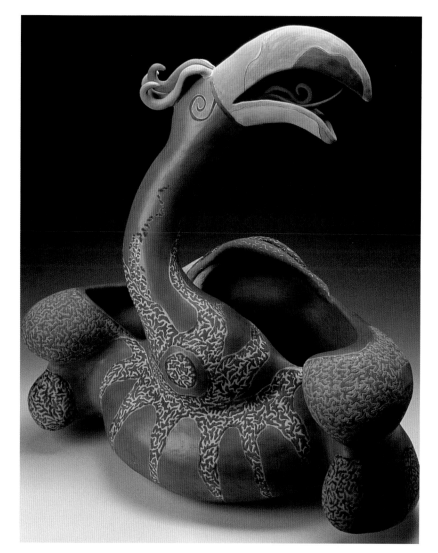

Marie-Elena Ottman

Two/Dos | 2004

25 X 27 X 14 INCHES (63.5 X 68.6 X 35.6 CM)

Coil-built earthenware; electric fired,
cone 03; slips, underglazes, sgraffito

PHOTO © GEOFFREY CARR PHOTOGRAPHY

Ceramic mementos and souvenirs can be found on countless fireplace mantles, in china cabinets and in store windows. Collections of ceramic animals carry surprisingly strong meanings through personal remembrance, imagination or perceived worth. —WW

Wendy Walgate
Red Toy Box | 2005

17 X 16 X 11 INCHES (43.2 X 40.6 X 27.9 CM)
Slip-cast white earthenware, porcelain; glaze, cone 06; vintage toy box
PHOTO © ARTIST

Silvie Granatelli

Swan Condiment Dish | 2000

4 X 3½ X 5 INCHES (10.2 X 8.9 X 12.7 CM)
Wheel-thrown, altered, and hand-built
porcelain; gas fired, cone 10
PHOTO © TIM BARNWELL

Linda A. Michalek

Untitled | 2003

10½ X 4½ X 4½ INCHES (26.7 X 11.4 X 11.4 CM)
Thrown and altered porcelain;
electric fired, cone 6; glazed

PHOTO © ARTIST

A custom-created raven feather brush was used to paint the black underglaze mark of the bird image. —GG

Glenn Grishkoff

Raven Brush Bouquet | 2005

15 X 24 X 9 INCHES (38.1 X 61 X 22.9 CM)

Wheel-thrown and coil-built porcelain; raku fired, cone 06; brush handles, coarse garnet dust, horse mane, deer tail

PHOTOS © MARK LAMOREAUX
COURTESY OF THE ART SPIRIT GALLERY OF FINE ART, COEUR D'ALENE, ID

Marlen Moggach

Mates | 2005

TALLEST, 9 X 4½ X 8½ INCHES (22.9 X 11.4 X 21.6 CM)

Wheel-thrown and hand-built raku clay;
cone 06; crackle glaze

PHOTOS © LAURENCE BRUNDRETT

Jeff Irwin

Woody II | 2004

23 X 13 X 9 INCHES (58.4 X 33 X 22.9 CM)

Slab- and coil-built earthenware; electric fired,
cone 03; glaze, cone 04

PHOTO © ARTIST

Echoing both mannerist art and the sculpture of Michael Lucero, color and imagery conspire in a poetic evocation of mood in Elizabeth F. Keller's expressive teapot. —JB

Elizabeth F. Keller

On the Side #3 (Seeing) | 2004

6½ X 10 X 8 INCHES (16.5 X 25.4 X 20.3 CM)

Slab-built buff stoneware; electric fired, cone 5; glaze, oil paint

PHOTOS © BILL EDMONDS

Kurt Weiser

Tiny Science | 2000

5½ X 5½ INCHES (14 X 14 CM)

Porcelain

PHOTO © CRAIG SMITH
COURTESY OF GARTH CLARK GALLERY, NY

Les Norton

Untitled | 2005

11 X 4½ X 4½ INCHES (27.9 X 11.4 X 11.4 CM)

Wheel thrown; reduction fired, cone 10; hand painted

PHOTO © ARTIST

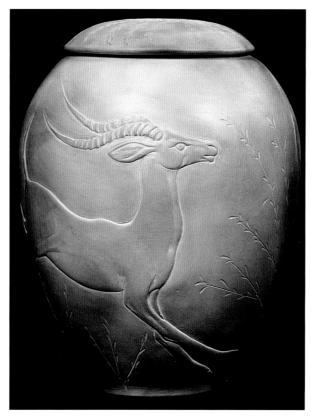

The elegant relief carving on Mary Ann Charette's pot is worthy of a pharaoh's tomb. The animal's dimensionality acts in symbiosis with the pot's expanding form. —JB

Mary Ann Charette

Leaping Impalas | 2005

8 X 6 INCHES (20.3 X 15.2 CM)
Wheel-thrown and carved porcelain;
electric fired, cone 04; smoked

PHOTO © PAUL ELBO

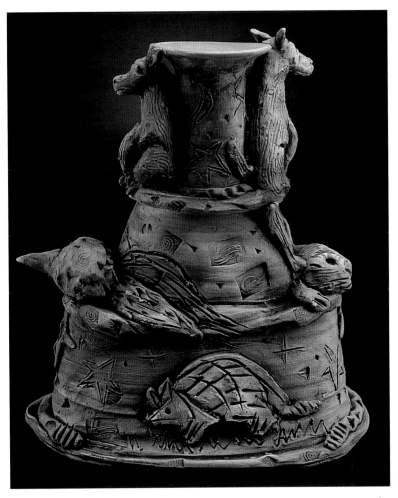

These critters seem to be escaping high water as they cling to their clay mastaba. Revealing something of his Louisiana home place, the vigor of Dennis Sipiorski's clay modeling captures the animals' angst. —JB

Dennis Sipiorski

Dogs, Rabbits, Snakes | 2001

36 X 20 X 8 INCHES (91.4 X 50.8 X 20.3 CM)
Thrown and hand-built red clay;
electric and salt fired, cone 6

PHOTO © ARTIST
COURTESY OF BRUNNER GALLERY

The effective simplicity of Howard Gerstein's Slug Mug *sounds distant echoes of the imagery from the movie* Dune, *whose protagonist might want this for his morning cup.* —JB

Howard Gerstein

Slug Mug | 1998

5 X 10⅝ X 3¼ INCHES (12.7 X 27 X 8.3 CM)

Slab-built stoneware; electric fired, cone 6

PHOTO © MONICA RIPLEY

It looks like this trickster rabbit has stolen the scene from her bovine cousin in Dawn Oakford's Over the Moon Teapot. *Naturalism and glaze treatment of fur conspire with cubistic exploration of form; it's the perfect teapot for an afternoon with L'albissola and Picasso.* —JB

Dawn Oakford

Over the Moon Teapot | n.d.

9 1/16 X 11 X 8 2/3 INCHES (23 X 28 X 22 CM)

Slip-cast stoneware; electric fired, 2300°F (1260°C); underglaze, clear glaze

PHOTOS © UFFE SCHULZE

Jim Budde's piece illustrates well Carl Jung's observation that an animal can be the symbolic Self—a reflection of our instinctive nature and its connected- ness with one's surroundings. —JB

Jim Budde

Taming the Shrew | 2002

23 X 18 X 8 INCHES (58.4 X 45.7 X 20.3 CM)

Slab-built stoneware; electric fired,
cone 3; glaze, cone 08

PHOTO © ARTIST

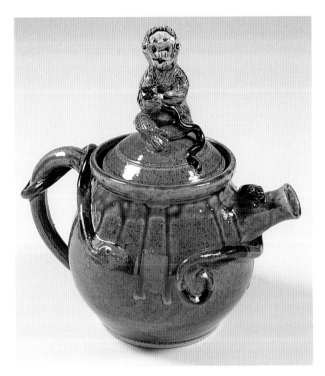

Crystal King

Monkey Snake Charmer Teapot | 2002

11 X 7 X 5 INCHES (27.9 X 17.8 X 12.7 CM)

Thrown clay with hand-built additions;
electric fired, cone 6; underglaze,
wood-ash dipped, celadon overglaze

PHOTO © PERRY ROACH

Bonnie Marie Smith

Monkey in a Tree | 2004

5 X 4 X 2½ INCHES (7.6 X 11.4 X 5.1 CM)

Hand-built earthenware; electric
fired, cone 04

PHOTO © ARTIST

Washington Ledesma's Coco exhibits a winning combination of the formal elements of variety and repetition in its animated surface pattern. —JB

Washington Ledesma

Coco | 2004

20 X 16 X 7 INCHES (50.8 X 40.6 X 17.8 CM)

Hand-built terra cotta; electric fired in oxidation, cone 02; underglazes, sgrafitto, matte finish

PHOTO © JERRY ANTHONY

Jeri Hollister

Tribute Series, Long Kawai, 04-04 | 2004

13 X 19 X 7 INCHES (33 X 48.3 X 17.8 CM)
Wheel-thrown, extruded, and slab-built earthenware;
electric fired, cone 03; iron oxide, glaze

PHOTO © ARTIST

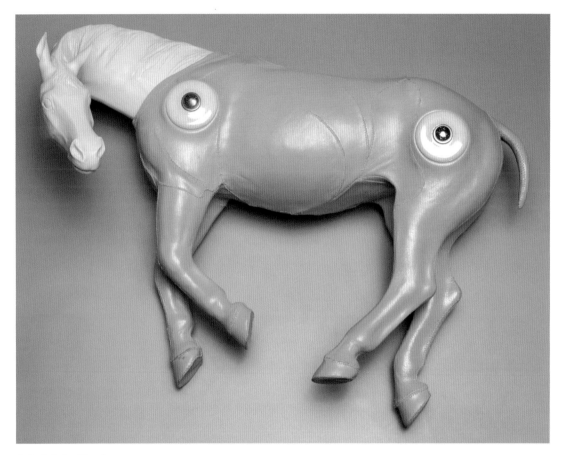

Adelaide Paul

Untitled | 2005

13 X 19½ INCHES (33 X 49.5 CM)

Porcelain; mixed media

PHOTO COURTESY OF GARTH CLARK GALLERY, NY

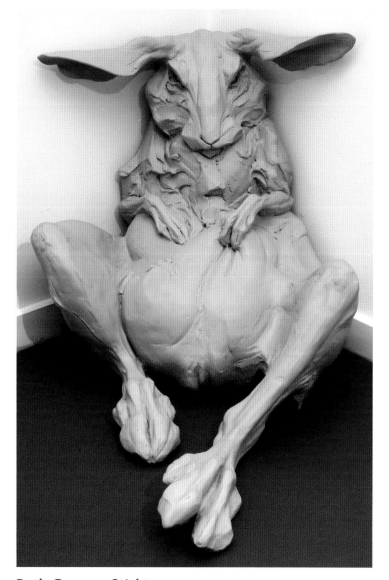

Beth Cavener Stichter

Strange Attraction | 2004

18 X 22 X 28 INCHES (45.7 X 55.9 X 71.1 CM)

Stoneware; bisque fired, cone 08; porcelain slip, cone 6

PHOTO © ARTIST
COURTESY OF SANDY BESSER

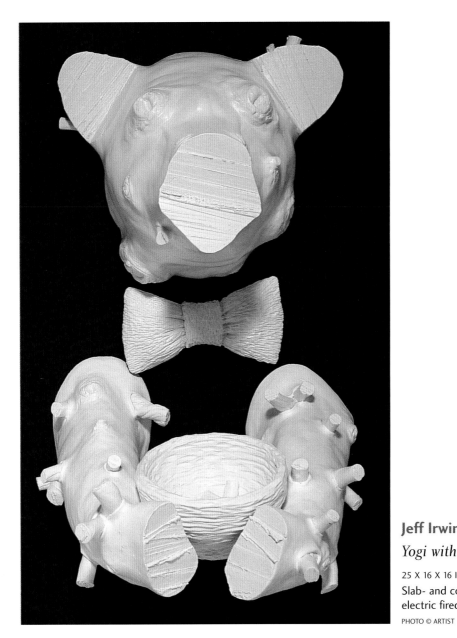

Jeff Irwin

Yogi with Begging Bowl | 2005

25 X 16 X 16 INCHES (63.5 X 40.6 X 40.6 CM)
Slab- and coil-built earthenware;
electric fired, cone 03; glaze, cone 04

PHOTO © ARTIST

David Regan

Eagle | 2003

19 X 21 X 9 INCHES (48.3 X 53.3 X 22.9 CM)

Porcelain

PHOTOS COURTESY OF GARTH CLARK GALLERY, NY

Pamela Earnshaw Kelly

Sheep III | 2000

29 X 18 X 7½ INCHES (73.7 X 45.7 X 19.1 CM)

Slab-built raku clay; raku fired, cone 05; glaze, patina

PHOTO © ARTIST

About the Juror

Artist and educator Joe Bova grew up in Texas in a family of outdoorsmen and learned much about animals from hunting and fishing. He has taught since 1969, most recently at Ohio University in Athens, Ohio. Bova is a professor emeritus of Louisiana State University. The recipient of national and regional fellowships, he has been a visiting artist at many schools, including New York State College of Ceramics at Alfred, University of Georgia's Cortona (Italy) program, Haystack Mountain School of Crafts in Maine, and Penland School of Crafts in North Carolina. His work is in many private and public collections, including the Los Angeles County Museum and the Mint Museum. A Fellow and Past President of the National Council on Education for the Ceramic Arts (NCECA), Bova was honored in 2006 with its Excellence in Teaching Award. He has two sons, Emil and Joseph. He and his wife, Linda Shafer, live with two dogs and two cats. Bova divides his time between home and studio in Santa Fe, New Mexico, and Athens, Ohio, where he continues to teach each spring.

Acknowledgments

With each subsequent call for entries in our 500 series, we here at Lark are delighted anew at the richness of contemporary ceramic work that is submitted. We are so fortunate to present it in this book, and grateful for the generosity of the many hundreds of artists who sent images. You have our deepest thanks for the opportunity to consider your work. Much appreciation also goes to Joe Bova, who broke away from his own busy life in the studio to jury the thousands of images and to write the introduction and commentaries on selected pieces.

Behind the scenes was the little "village" of Lark staffers who helped bring this book into being. I want to thank our crack editorial team, animal lovers, all: Dawn Dillingham, Rosemary Kast, Nathalie Mornu, and interns Megan Taylor Cox and Sue Stigleman. Jackie Kerr designed the book and made it flow beautifully (thanks!). Finally, this book could not have been realized without the top-notch production work of art department whizzes Shannon Yokeley and Jeff Hamilton.

Suzanne J.E. Tourtillott

Contributing Artists

Karen Adelaar
Hopewell Junction, New York
Page 159

Pavel G. Amromin
Gainesville, Florida
Pages 230, 248

Cheryl Andrews
Asheville, North Carolina
Pages 320, 349

Chris Antemann
Joseph, Oregon
Page 293

Tré Arenz
Deceased
Pages 151, 169, 246, 286

Adrian Arleo
Lolo, Montana
Page 13

Elissa Armstrong
Lawrence, Kansas
Pages 69, 262, 291

Robin Sadek Ascher
Scarsdale, New York
Page 350

Renee Audette
Gainesville, Florida
Pages 119, 265

Debra Bacianga
Seattle, Washington
Pages 105, 318

Marian Baker
Yarmouth, Maine
Page 363

Susan Bell
Austin, Texas
Page 348

Brenda Bennett
Gladstone, Australia
Page 18

Anne Bernard-Pattis
Highland Park, Illinois
Page 323

Clinton Berry
St. Louis, Missouri
Page 80

Chris Berti
Urbana, Illinois
Page 140

Susanna Birley
Chalford, United Kingdom
Pages 168, 220

Suzy Birstein
Vancouver, British Columbia, Canada
Pages 39, 342

Rebekah Bogard
Reno, Nevada
Pages 173, 201, 296

Susie Bogard
Golden, Colorado
Pages 155, 280

Elaine Bolz
Corrales, New Mexico
Pages 272, 344

Anne-Beth Borselius
Hammenhog, Sweden
Pages 84, 380

Susan Bostwick
Edwardsville, Illinois
Pages 51, 67, 281, 331

Skuja Braden
Meadow Vista, California
Page 242

Pamela H. Brewer
Banner Elk, North Carolina
Page 224

Cynthia Bringle
Penland, North Carolina
Pages 31, 215

Jim Budde
Boise, Idaho
Pages 241, 302, 410

John Byrd
New York, New York
Pages 249, 317, 325

Gary Carlos
San Leandro, California
Page 103

Scott Causey
Sarasota, Florida
Pages 40, 340

Mary Ann Charette
Bethesda, Maryland
Pages 100, 106, 406

Mark Chatterley
Williamston, Michigan
Page 116

Jennie Chien
Nyack, New York
Page 276

Tim Christensen-Kirby
Milton, New Hampshire
Pages 239, 362, 388

Lisa Clague
Bakersville, North Carolina
Pages 229, 303, 333

Elizabeth Coleman
Marquette, Michigan
Pages 256, 268

Cris Conklin
Boulder, Colorado
Page 362

Kelly Connole
Northfield, Minnesota
Cover, page 15

Cynthia Consentino
Northampton, Massachusetts
Pages 75, 76, 334

David Cooke
Huddersfield, West Yorkshire, United Kingdom
Pages 22, 393

Jaimie Cooney
Rimbey, Alberta, Canada
Pages 68, 93

Karen Copensky
Blairstown, New Jersey
Pages 29, 31, 32, 150

Annette Corcoran
Pacific Grove, California
Pages 87, 297, 364

Linda Cordell
Philadelphia, Pennsylvania
Pages 205, 211

Salinda Dahl
Siler City, North Carolina
Page 255

Andrew Davis
Mt. Pleasant, Michigan
Page 133

Lindsey de Ovies
Issy Les Moulineaux, France
Page 352

Laura DeAngelis
Kansas City, Missouri
Pages 156, 164, 372

Maria DeCastro
Fallbrook, California
Page 288

Nancy Dimock
Tucson, Arizona
Page 53

Gary Dinnen
Sacramento, California
Page 244

Liza Domeier
Nicollet, Minnesota
Page 228

Patrick L. Dougherty
Bellevue, Kentucky
Pages 82, 204

Caroline Douglas
Boulder, Colorado
Page 218

Jane Dunsmore
Frederick, Maryland
Page 129

Emily Dyer
Minneapolis, Minnesota
Page 330

Anne Fallis Elliott
New York, New York
Page 37

Melody Ellis
Edwardsville, Illinois
Pages 41, 104, 304

Mary Engel
Athens, Georgia
Page 243

Pamela Epperson
Chapel Hill, North Carolina
Page 64

Michelle Erickson
New York, New York
Page 386

Bill Evans
Seattle, Washington
Pages 11, 16, 394

Rena Fafalios
New York, New York
Page 149

France Fauteux
Quebec, Quebec, Canada
Page 59

Laszlo Fekete
New York, New York
Page 195

Kenneth Ferguson
New York, New York
Pages 81, 177

Ilena Finocchi
North Lima, Ohio
Pages 120, 314

Kate Fisher
Denton, Texas
Pages 85, 254, 360

Debbie Fong
Richmond, California
Pages 14, 234

Peggy Forman
Portola Valley, California
Page 309

Michael Fromme
Springfield, Oregon
Page 382

Michelle C. Gallagher
Portland, Oregon
Page 146

Howard Gerstein
Somerville, Massachusetts
Pages 223, 408

Bruce Gholson
Seagrove, North Carolina
Pages 88, 101, 107

Diane Gilbert
Columbia, South Carolina
Page 27

Daphne Gillen
Redwood Valley, California
Pages 235, 275

Genya Glass
Richmond, Virginia
Pages 269, 347

Ann Gleason
Tryon, North Carolina
Pages 312, 379

Marta Matray Gloviczki
Rochester, New Mexico
Page 206

Amy Goldstein-Rice
Inman, South Carolina
Page 253

Frank A. Gosar
Eugene, Oregon
Page 226

Silvie Granatelli
Floyd, Virginia
Pages 28, 345, 398

Leslie Green
Philomath, Oregon
Page 61

Susan Greenleaf
Washington, D.C.
Pages 66, 310

Bruce Grimes
Cedarville, Ohio
Pages 60, 382

Glenn Grishkoff
Anaheim, California
Pages 311, 400

Stefani Gruenberg
Los Angeles, California
Page 94

Susan Halls
Easthampton, Massachusetts
Pages 135, 148, 271

Nancy Halter
Billings, Montana
Page 383

Kevin B. Hardin
Tulsa, Oklahoma
Pages 25, 134, 227

Wes Harvey
Lubbock, Texas
Pages 43, 56

Priscilla Heep
New York, New York
Page 183

Carrianne Hendrickson
Buffalo, New York
Pages 161, 326, 369

Samantha Henneke
Seagrove, North Carolina
Pages 88, 97

Annemie Heylen
Keerbergen, Belgium
Page 179

Bryan Hiveley
Miami, Florida
Pages 5, 341, 361

Reynold Ho
Montebello, California
Page 178

Bev Hogg
Hackett, Australian Capital Territory, Australia
Page 132

Norman D. Holen
Minneapolis, Minnesota
Pages 55, 182

Jeri Hollister
Ann Arbor, Michigan
Pages 209, 413

Keri Huber
White Bear Lake, Minnesota
Page 58

James Ibur
St. Louis, Missouri
Page 122

Steve Irvine
Wiarton, Ontario, Canada
Page 170

Jeff Irwin
San Diego, California
Pages 402, 416

Roxanne Jackson
Portland, Oregon
Page 231

Nan Jacobsohn
Sparta, Tennessee
Pages 138, 203

Greg Jahn
Billings, Montana
Page 383

Rytas Jakimavičius
Vilnius, Lithuania
Pages 251, 295, 356

Kerry Jameson
London, United Kingdom
Pages 17, 26, 233

Hwang Jeng-daw
Tainan, Taiwan
Page 345

Deborah Johnston
Toronto, Ontario, Canada
Page 25

Delyth Jones
London, United Kingdom
Pages 144, 315, 328

Mary Jordan
Auroa, Illinois
Page 147

Irianna Kanellopoulou
Victoria, Australia
Page 175

Phyllis A. Kaye
Los Angeles, California
Page 328

Elizabeth F. Keller
Conway, South Carolina
Pages 162, 403

Pamela Earnshaw Kelly
Montrose, Pennsylvania
Pages 70, 95, 124, 260, 327, 418

Beth Kennedy
Bozeman, Montana
Page 38

Mary E. Kershaw
West Sussex, United Kingdom
Page 73

Crystal King
Asheboro, North Carolina
Page 411

Annette Kirma
Beaverton, Oregon
Pages 322, 336

Nina G. Koepcke
San Jose, California
Page 192

Jim Koudelka
Portland, Oregon
Page 336

Karl Kuhns
Dolgeville, New York
Pages 196, 366

Sylvia Lampen
Roswell, Georgia
Page 130